ELDER AN ᴛʜɪᴍᴏꜱ

OF SAINT ANNE'S

**The wise and God-bearing contemporary
Father of Athos**

by Dr Charalambos M. Bousias

Translated by Fr Nicholas Palis
Revised and edited by Fr Joseph Frawley

Orthodox Logos Publishing

Front cover:
Elder Anthimos of Saint Anne's (1913 - 1996)
Photo by Douglas Lyttle

Greek original title:

ΔΡΟΣ ΧΑΡΑΛΑΜΠΟΥΣ Μ. ΜΠΟΥΣΙΑ
Ο ΓΕΡΩΝ ΑΝΘΙΜΟΣ Ο ΑΓΙΑΝΝΑΝΙΤΗΣ
ΕΚΔΟΣΕΙΣ ΜΥΓΔΟΝΙΑ
ΘΕΣΣΑΛΟΝΙΚΗ 2004

© **Theophileon Brotherhood**
P.O.Box 12
63087 Daphni, Mount Athos
Greece
E-mail: theophileon@otenet.gr

© 2011, **Orthodox Logos Publishing,** The Netherlands
www.orthodoxlogos.com

ISBN: 978-90-811555-6-4

An iconographic portrait of
Elder Anthimos of Saint Anne's
painted by iconographer Marios Pelelis.

APOLYTIKION TONE 3
Special Melody: "Thy Confession of the Divine Faith"

With all reverence, let us praise Anthimos, who in our own time dawned over Athos like a star shedding a new light of piety as a brightly shining vessel of grace, bearing the undoubted flower of purity, with great love crying out to him: "As one who rejoices with the angels, ever entreat Christ for us."

KONTAKION PLAGAL TONE 4
Special Melody: "O Victorious Leader"

As a most enlightened and inspired ascetic, a follower of the way of stillness and wakefulness, let us praise the newly planted yet undoubted fragrant Flower of the Holy Mountain, a Rose of the great Skete of Saint Anne, with great love crying out, "Hail, most wise Anthimos"

MEGALYNARION

As one who kept the Lord's commandments, and the guiding Star of love in practice, the very standard of the spirit-bearing Fathers newly shining forth in Athos, let us celebrate Anthimos in song.

CONTENTS

5

IV. PRACTICAL PATERNAL COUNSELS

V. ELDER ANTHIMOS AS SEEN BY HIS CONTEMPORARIES

Letter of the Ecumenical Patriarch

To the most venerable erudite Archimandrite Cherubim Apostolou, Elder of the Brotherhood of the Theophileon at Saint Anne, beloved child of our Modesty in the Lord, grace and peace from God.

With joy we received from your Venerableness the piously submitted work of the most erudite Dr Charalambos Bousias entitled *Elder Anthimos of Saint Anne's*.

Therefore, through this Patriarchal Letter, we proceed to thank you fervently for sending this work which depicts the venerable figure of the ever-memorable Spiritual Father Elder Anthimos. Congratulating you from our heart, we very eagerly bestow our paternal and Patriarchal blessing, invoking upon your Venerableness and those brethren practicing asceticism with you God's grace and His infinite mercy.

December 11, 2000

+ Bartholomew of Constantinople,
your fervent intercessor before God

Prologue

Our age is an age of apostasy from God's will. It is an age of disobedience, of the kingdom of egotism, of the kingdom of lewdness, of sinful pleasure, of disbelief, of easy profit, of profiteering. However, in this age, as always, God has His own people, people whose speech is "seasoned with salt" (Col. 4:6). They make the area around them, and all of society in general, savory. Let us not forget the observation of the Apostle Paul in his Epistle to the Romans, "where sin abounded, grace much more abounded" (Rom. 5:20). We feel this grace, which descends like the dew of Hermon from the heavenly peaks to the people, especially in our sin-loving age. In recent times, this grace refreshed holy men, who by word and by works made faith firm and magnified the name which is above every name, that of our Savior Christ. It is worth mentioning some ascetic personalities with the gifts of foreknowledge and clairvoyance: Father Iakovos in Euboia, Father Porphyrios in Attica, and Father Paisios on Athos; the wise missionaries Amphilochios of Patmos and Philotheos of Paros; the good Levite Demetrios Gagastathis in Platano of Trikala; the Spiritual Fathers of the cities, Epiphanios and Agathangelos in Athens, Athanasios in Amarousion and Simon in Penteli. We must also mention the erudite and spirit-moved Joel in Kalamata and Gerasimos of Little Saint Anne's; and finally, the hesychasts and Spiritual Fathers of the Holy Mountain, Joseph the Cave-Dweller, Ephraim of Katounakia, Gabriel of Dionysiou and Anthimos of Saint Anne's.

All these were habitations of the virtues and fragrances of the All-Holy Spirit, from Whom they received grace to gladden the souls of the living Christian flock. All these personalities, along with many others, both known and unknown, are the gift of our Lord to contemporary society. They are the yeast which leavens the small dough of the pious pleroma.

Elder Anthimos had many gifts, which he diligently hid. He was distinguished by humility, meekness and his vast love, virtues which he obtained with many struggles and harsh ascesis. He was prudent, chaste, discerning, hospitable, a loving Father who emptied himself in order to fill the souls of others, and those of his brothers, in whom he saw our Lord Himself, Who said, "Whatever you have done for one of the least of these my brethren, you have done for me" (Matt. 25:40). When everyone despaired because of the trials and the difficulties they encountered, he had absolute trust in God and remained calm. He held the hand of his visitors and took their pulse. He became as one with them, imparting his meekness and his peace, the gifts of the Holy Spirit with which he had been adorned after many years of ascesis.

Elder Anthimos was particularly characterized by his praying heart. He had the gift of correct guidance, and also much diverse knowledge, which he revealed, not so that others would admire him, but to draw and comfort even his most demanding and difficult listeners. Everyone listened to him with admiration, and the grace of the Lord which dwelt in him unlocked the hearts of those who had cast off the old man, were renewed, and proceeded on the path of the new life "in Christ."

The spiritual depth of Elder Anthimos and the wealth of his wisdom became more obvious with his ascetical experience, and in the way he faced various circumstances.

Everyone admired the purity of his face with his sparkling blue eyes, his concentration and vigilance, the calm and correct way he reacted, and his always accurate answers interspersed with sayings of the ancient philosophers, the holy Fathers of our Church, and Scriptural passages. He was an example for abbots, monks and lay people to imitate.

The present work wishes to emphasize that "Jesus Christ is the same yesterday and today and forever" (Heb. 13:8), presenting the great ascetical personality of the "wise" and "God-bearing" Elder Anthimos, as he has been called by other contemporary Athonite Fathers, who are themselves wise and God-bearing. For the past year we have visited various persons who were acquainted with the blessed Elder, or who had wondrous experiences of him. With our weak antennae, and with our small powers, we have compiled and documented a few of them. We did not spare any efforts, but ran all over Greece like honeybees in order to harvest the sweetest nectar of the experiences and the miracles of Father Anthimos. We went alone, or as directed by, or in the company of Elder Cherubim Apostolou, the Elder's successor in the Kalyva of the Entrance of the Theotokos of the Skete of Saint Anne. All these show, even deficiently, who the blessed Elder was, he who lived "wisely and righteously and devoutly" (Tit. 2:12), purifying himself and becoming pleasing to God and his fellow man.

Dr Charalambos M. Bousias
January 2000

13

Introduction to the English edition

Mount Athos, the Holy Mountain, the Garden of the Most Holy Theotokos, has been a source of inspiration for Orthodox Christians for more than a thousand years. It offers a salutary antidote to the turbulent storm of modern existence, revealing the way of holiness to Christians in every land, and in every walk of life.

Throughout the centuries, Orthodox pilgrims from various countries have visited the Holy Mountain to refresh themselves at this spiritual oasis in the midst of the desert of contemporary secularism and ungodliness. Many Orthodox Christians around the world dream of making this pilgrimage and setting foot on the sacred soil of Athos. Perhaps, as they begin to walk up the path from the shore, they may recall the words of Psalm 23/24:3-4, which are chanted during the Third Antiphon at Liturgy for the Feast of the Transfiguration of the Lord: "Who shall ascend the mountain of the Lord, and who shall stand in His holy place? He who is guiltless (athoos) in his hands and pure in his heart..."

Other people who may wish to travel to the Holy Mountain will never have the opportunity to do so. They must be content to read about the Holy Mountain and its inhabitants in soul-profiting books such as this one on the Life of the ever-memorable Elder Anthimos.

Why is Athos considered holy? It is holy because it was given to the Mother of God as her portion. She told St Peter of Athos (June 12) that she had chosen Mount Athos to be a habitation for those who wish to fight against the devil, and promised to be an invincible ally and helper in their struggle. Furthermore, she promised to provide for their physical and spiritual well-being during their lifetime. After their death, she would entreat her Son and God to grant full pardon for their sins to those who lived and died in repentance, and would also request Him to number them among His saints.

Like all Athonite monks, Fr Anthimos had a deep devotion to the Mother of God. The church of his Kalyva is dedicated to the Feast of her Entrance into the Temple (November 21), the day on which he received the monastic tonsure. Reference is made in the Biography (Chapter 9, "The Elder's Love of the All-Holy Virgin") to several wonderworking icons of the Most Holy Theotokos on Mount Athos. Consolation at Vatopedi (January 21), Directress at Xenophontou (June 20, January 21), Fearful Protection at Koutloumousiou (Bright Tuesday), Hope of the Hopeless at Vatopedi, Quick to Hear at Docheiariou (November 9, Oct. 1), Sweet-Kissing at Philotheou (March 27, May 14 and Thomas Sunday), Refuge and Protection, etc.

The Holy Mountain has long been regarded as the defender of the purity and fullness of Orthodox doctrine, and its zealous saints as models of true piety. One of Fr Anthimos's greatest virtues was his strictness, or exactitude, in matters of the Orthodox Faith. This is important, because one cannot be a saint without being Orthodox in faith. In the early Church, heretics who were put to death because of their faith in Christ were not honored as martyrs or saints, because they did not confess the truth in all its fullness. Christ said to the Samaritan woman: "You worship what you do not know", but the Jews, He said, worship God "in spirit and in truth" (John 4:22-23). We are also called to discern and confess the truth in order to inherit the heavenly Kingdom. That is why Fr Anthimos was so insistent that correct doctrine is essential for those who struggle for salvation.

The story of Abba Piammon in St John Cassian's Conferences (18:5) states that Christ lived in a community with His disciples. In a similar way, monks live in a community under the direction of an Elder, or an Igumen. Cenobitic and eremitic monasticism began around the third century, and saints such as St Basil the Great (January 1) and St Pachomios (May 15) laid down special Rules, or principles of monastic life.

Many women have also embraced this life of spiritual struggle in order to cleanse themselves from passions and vices, and to acquire the virtues. St Anthony the Great (January 17) entrusted his younger sister to a community of "well known and faithful virgins" who had devoted themselves to Christ (St Athanasios, *Life Of Saint Anthony*, Ch. 3). The nun Kassiane, who was the first cousin of Fr Anthimos, also lived the angelic life of monasticism, and was filled with the gifts of the Holy Spirit. She knew beforehand the day of her death, and sent word to her nephew to make preparations for her funeral.

This biography is not merely a chronicle of the life of the ever-memorable Father Anthimos; it is also a picture of monastic life on the Holy Mountain. In broader terms, *The Life Of Elder Anthimos* is about the life of every Christian, which ought to be directed towards God rather than the things of this world. We must realize that we cannot simply remain as we are now, for we are all called to become saints. In order to attain this goal, we must engage in spiritual struggle (ascesis), purifying ourselves from every sin which separates us from God, while acquiring every virtue which leads to holiness.

At Baptism we were enlisted as "warriors of Christ", and our battle is against the world, our own fallen nature, and the demons. The cross we wear is a reminder of the Savior's words, "Take up your cross and follow me." Those who do not take up their cross are not worthy of Him (Matt. 10:38, 16:24).

God commands everyone to be perfect or holy, which amounts to the same thing (Deut. 18:13, Matt. 5:48, Eph. 4:11-13, Col. 1:28, 4:12, James 1:4). "If thou wouldst be perfect, go and sell everything that thou hast and give it to the poor, and then thou shalt have treasure in heaven, and come and follow me". (Matt. 19:21).

Purification from the passions and triumph over vice are necessary in order for us to acquire the virtues and to grow more and more into the divine likeness. We are all created in God's image (i.e. we are endowed with reason, free will, and self-determination). The divine likeness in man, however, may become distorted through sin. This likeness can be cleansed and restored, not solely through our feeble efforts, but with God's help (John 15:5, Matt. 7:7).

Holiness is the true goal of our spiritual striving. If it were not possible to attain this goal, then it would be unreasonable for God to command, "Be holy" (Lev. 11:44, Lev. 19:1-2, Lev. 20:7-8, 1 Peter 1:16). God wills that we become holy, which is the destiny of all people who are living in this world (I Thess. 4:3), whether monastics or laity.

17

Submission to Elders

More than once in this book, novices are said to obey their Elders with unquestioning obedience. Perhaps some explanation is required, lest people who are not well acquainted with the Orthodox ascetical and spiritual tradition form a mistaken impression. One of the most difficult things for contemporary secular people to understand is why monks would voluntarily renounce their own will and promise complete obedience to an Elder or Spiritual Father. Perhaps this seems incomprehensible because many people today do not feel obliged to obey any laws at all, whether civil or religious.

A monk entering a monastery is assigned a Spiritual Father who trains and instructs him in the monastic life. One of the first things the novice learns is to cut off his own will and submit to his Elder in all matters without question, without opposition or rebellion. This is not an unhealthy control or manipulation of an individual by unscrupulous cult leaders, nor does it make the novice blind or brain -washed. The novice voluntarily defers to the Elder's wisdom and experience, while distrusting his own judgment. As St John Climacus explains, "Obedience is an abandonment of discernment in a wealth of discernment" (*Ladder* 4:3).

Why should the novice mistrust his own judgment? Because our minds are defiled and darkened by the body (*Ladder* 14:28). Obedience leads to humility and dispassion (Step 4:55, 4:71, 25:62, 26:72). Obedience helps the monk to avoid disobedience and conceit (Step 4:55, 56, and Step 25) as well as delusion.

Christ did not seek His own will, but that of His Father (John 5:30, 6:38). Christ's will is not opposed to the Father's will, but is in harmony with it. A novice struggles to reject his own will and understanding, trusting in his Elder's greater knowledge and experience. The Elder's will, insofar as he has purified himself of the passions and has acquired the virtues, is in harmony with God's will. This is why the monastic literature says that the novice is to obey his Elder just as he would obey God. Fr Anthimos became a sure guide for others because his obedience to his own Elder enabled him to acquire knowledge and discernment in his spiritual life.

Father Anthimos

There are twenty monasteries, twelve sketes, and many small hermitages on the Holy Mountain. St Anne's Skete lies almost at the tip of the thirty-five mile long Chalkidike peninsula on which the monasteries of Mount Athos are located.

Fr Anthimos came to read in the libraries of Mount Athos, but did not intend to remain there as a monk. He asked himself why people would choose to live in such a remote place under such difficult conditions. Monastics flee the world in order to remove themselves from worldly ties and influences. The deserts and forests where they build their cells are not just remote and tranquil places which are conducive to prayer. There is also danger from wild animals, from a harsh climate, as well as from the attacks of demons. There must be something worthwhile here, he reasoned. So there was. There on the Holy Mountain he found the Pearl of great price (Matt. 13:46).

Fr Anthimos was instructed in the "science of sciences" by his Elder Father Gabriel, and he passed this knowledge on to his own disciples. He represents only one link in the unbroken chain of spiritual wisdom passed down from Elder to disciple for more than a thousand years.

The ever-memorable Elder Paisios told Fr Anthimos's disciple and successor Fr Cherubim to take notes of everything that Elder Anthimos said. Similarly, the *Sayings of the desert Fathers* were compiled by disciples of various God-bearing Elders in order to preserve them for future generations of monks.

Their authority came from the example they set in fulfilling the commandments of God. Many times they would not offer their own teaching, but would cite the words of the Fathers and saints of the Church instead. The fifth century writer Sozomen said that monks did not demonstrate virtue through persuasive arguments, but by their own example (*Church History* 1:2). Therefore, when they did give instruction to others, it had the power to heal the spiritual infirmities of those who were disposed to hear it.

Elder Anthimos did not try to force people to obey him. Sometimes he would give in to others, as on the occasion when a certain dentist wished to take his photograph, but Fr Anthimos did not want him to do so. When the picture was printed, everything in the background could be seen quite distinctly, but the Elder did not come out.

Fr Anthimos, „the flower of St Anne's," and "the new boast of St Anne's Skete", was a great model of prayer and fasting. It should not be surprising that he also worked miracles and was clairvoyant. After all, the Lord said, "He who believes in me will also do the works that I do; and he will do greater works than these... (John 14:12). Christ Himself links prayer and fasting with spiritual gifts (Mark 9:29). In our evil and sinful times, however, it may be a greater miracle to save one's soul than to raise the dead.

In *The Life of Elder Anthimos* we find confirmation of the teachings of Christ, and the fulfillment of His promises. Living in a monastery and receiving the monastic tonsure are not, by themselves, indications of a saintly life. Today's monks are called to measure themselves against the saints of the past, and to attain a similar degree of holiness. Those of us who live "in the world" are also called to do the very same thing. The Church must not only look back to its heroes of the distant past as examples of holiness, but must continue to produce new saints until the Lord comes again. This is both a goal and a challenge for the present generation of Athonite monks, and for all of us. In spite of the current state of the world, it is still possible to attain such holiness. The life of Fr Anthimos demonstrates that this is so.

Archpriest Joseph Frawley
St Martin's Chapel, West Point, NY
October 2010

I.
Biography

Dawn in Zireia

The small village of Kallianoi is located in the heights of the Corinthian land, in the peaks of the cloud-covered Zireia. At a height of seven hundred meters, a little before the lake of Stymphalia, where the mythical Hercules killed the Stymphalian birds, and opposite the village of Psari, the birthplace of New Martyr Nicholas (beheaded at Constantinople on February 14, 1554), Kallianoi has resisted time, which tames everything. Although it is the main village of the surrounding area, today it has few inhabitants, for most of them went to Kiato, Corinth and Athens hoping for better days. Its natural resources are small, and the struggle to survive is difficult for its inhabitants.

In this semi-mountainous and semi-barren village the little Constantine Zapheiropoulos, who later became the famous Spiritual Father Anthimos of St Anne's, first saw the light of the sun.

His first cries were heard on November 5, 1913, which with his premature orphanhood, the harsh conditions of life and his subsequent voluntary ascesis and prayer which ended in contrition, would accompany him in all his later life. These things, however, gave him the unending joy and rejoicing of the Kingdom of Heaven. His parents

Charalambos and Vasiliki took him in their arms and hugged their young offspring in their embrace, but did not manage to see his godly progress, because He quickly called them to Himself. His father Charalambos was from a famous family which had come to Kallianoi from the mountains of Arcadia. His mother was from Kallianoi. Both were pious and virtue-loving, especially Constantine's mother. She was quickly "taken up, so that wickedness would not change her prudence" (Wisdom of Solomon 4:11), leaving him orphaned at the age of seven, together with Anastasios, his only brother in the flesh. Their estate was modest. One could characterize them as poor, since their daily bread came with difficulty out of the fields which belonged to them. Although poor in land estates, they were rich, however, in love of God. They unstintingly passed this love on to their children also, especially to Constantine, a zealot for the Forerunner's way of life.

Vasiliki's premature death plunged the father and the two boys into very deep mourning, which became unbearable for the two young lads after their father's second marriage. Not only did their stepmother never love them, but she also beat them without mercy. The two orphans had no place in their paternal home. The nest which warmed them now became a scorpion's nest, and a warm embrace was replaced by savage beatings with a stick. Their stepmother's harsh and coarse behavior made even the little children's sleep difficult. She lived an immoral life and did not want the children to see her iniquitous actions. One day she attempted to kill little Anastasios, who escaped due to the sudden return of their father. Another time she tried to burn the two children in the oven, where the poor things took refuge to warm their emaciated and frozen little bodies.

After all these things, Constantine decided to leave secretly and to seek his fate on his own. He took all his belongings in a handkerchief: two changes of clothes and a piece of bread with a little food, and set out. He made the Sign of the Cross and took to the road. He stopped at the edge of the village to look back and gaze at his little village which could not contain him now. Pictures from the happy years with his beloved dear mother came back to his mind, even if they were poor. He was certain that she would escort him and guide him from heaven on his new journey to the unknown. He called upon her, and a burning tear rolled down his soft childlike cheeks. He did not go very far. He sought refuge in the neighboring Nemea, where he worked hard in a grocery store in order to have food and shelter. There he became acquainted with a certain Athonite Elder, who approached him and took him to Athens with him.

Acquaintance with Famous Spiritual Fathers

Constantine finished the Academy in the city of light and letters, and since he loved letters very much, he frequented various libraries and read with unceasing zeal. Our good God, his only company and consolation, opened new paths for him. He Who said, "Seek first the Kingdom of Heaven and all these shall be added unto you" (Matt. 6:33) was interested in and concerned for the adolescent who had been orphaned on earth, but not in heaven. He brought him to the virtuous Spiritual Father Jerome of St Paul's, an unerring guide who stood by him and led him on the paths of the divine commandments and of salvation, to the living waters "springing up to eternal life" (John 4:14). Fr Jerome's vigils, his ceaseless prayer of the heart, "Lord Jesus Christ, have mercy on me, a sinner", his fasts and every type of hardship of his body, his love for everyone, his elevating humility and the multitude of his virtues, by God's grace, made him an experienced and clairvoyant Spiritual Father.

Divine providence placed him in young Constantine's path, to form his easily malleable heart according to the eternal will of the heavenly Father. Later, when Fr Jerome was deprived of natural light because of a serious disease of his eyes, he received an increase of spiritual light from the Light-giving Lord, and he received the gift of clairvoyance until the end of his life on earth. When Fr Jerome's physical powers weakened and he could not guide young Constantine, whom he saw progressing in Christ, with the eyes of his clairvoyance, he sent him to the famous Spiritual Father Michael the Blind who lived in the small hermitage of the Holy Archangels in Vyrona.

Elder Michael was from Madyton of Eastern Thrace. He was the brother of the famous Spiritual Father Gabriel Lambi, a monk of the Skete of St Anne on Mt Athos. Michael also lived in God-pleasing asceticism in this large Skete's Kalyva of the Entrance of the Theotokos for more than two decades. During these years he worked diligently, prayed with contrition, labored honorably in asceticism and was an obedient disciple. He became a model of monastic life and a precious vessel of the gifts of the Holy Spirit. However, for reasons which only the Lord knows and permits, his eyes were assailed by an illness which gradually made him completely blind. So he was forced to come out into the world for therapy, and there to carry the cross of the sins of many souls who trusted him as a Spiritual Father and unerring guide toward salvation. Although he himself was blind, he scattered the true light, the unsetting light of Christ, to souls who lived in the darkness of ignorance and of sin-loving daily life.

Due to his blindness, Fr Michael did not serve as a priest in the hermitage of the Holy Archangels in Vyrona. He did not yet have the gift of speech for preaching. He was content simply with the work of hearing Confessions, and with the admission of sins and the correct guidance of the believers. It was not rare for someone to wait quite a while for his turn to come for Confession. No matter how weary he was, Fr Michael tirelessly and patiently heard everyone. He had great love, understanding, and discretion. Everyone felt comfortable at his epitrachelion, and left feeling renewed and joyous. For this reason he had gathered so many people around him that they crowded in the small, but for them redeeming church of his hermitage. The Elder knew how to cultivate the field of the soul of the penitents quietly, speaking to them about the works of virtue, repentance, tears, prayer, charity and ascesis. Through his humble work, he guided souls freed from the bonds of sin to Paradise guilelessly, humbly, without selfishness and with firm steps.

In Fr Michael's quiet and poor cell where people found consolation and strengthening at his epitrachelion during those difficult years of expatriation and misfortune, Constantine also took refuge as if it were a calm port. He was intoxicated by the aroma of the Athonite wilderness which the blind Elder breathed, and his love for reading books in the rich libraries of the Holy Mountain urged him to visit them. He pictured Athos as a spiritual oasis, as indeed it is, a piece of the heavenly Eden transplanted onto the long, narrow peninsula of the Macedonian land, which the Panagia selected as her portion, and which for centuries has been watered by the sweat and the tears of the firm-souled ascetics. Fr Michael not only cultivated this longing of the young Constantine, but also, at the appropriate moment, sent him to his brother Gabriel, who lived an ascetical life there in a God-pleasing manner, so that he might take care of him and direct him on the Athonite footpaths.

The Young Constantine's Arrival on Athos

The Kallianote, who loved to read, took the road for the Athonite life when he had scarcely completed his seventeenth year. "I did not come here with the desire to become a monk", he said, "but to read books from the inexhaustible libraries of the Cenobia and the Sketes of the Mountain."

At the Skete of St Anne and in the Kalyva of the Entrance of the Theotokos, of the familiar Brotherhood of the Theophileon, Constantine met Elders Theophilos and Gabriel, who received him with abundant unselfish and unhypocritical love. Constantine, who was eagerly initiated by them into the secrets of monastic conduct and life, particularly admired this. Although it was not his goal to become a monk, nevertheless he philosophized every day about the life of these otherworldly inhabitants of the wilderness. In the beginning he asked himself, "Why should these Fathers live in these inaccessible cliffs and kalyvas? Why should they, like wilderness-loving sparrows, build the nests of their asceticism in the shady forest, and even on the dry slopes of the cloud-covered Athos? Why should they ceaselessly give their weak flesh over to hardship, scorning the joys and the beauties of the world?"

With the passage of time, these unanswered questions, which the Tempter poses to every newcomer to the Holy Mountain, ceased in Constantine's soul, and the grace of God fully answered him. In 1929, the Skete of St Anne numbered two hundred and seventy Fathers. The young lover of reading, with the correct guidance of his Elders, slowly came to feel an aversion for the vanity of secular pleasures. He rejoiced for the eternity of the incorruptible good things (1 Peter 1:4) "prepared from the foundation of the world" (Matt. 25:34). He also would go to the vigils in the Kyriakon of St Anne, and was literally overcome by the slow nocturnal chants he had never heard before, and something within him urged him to dedicate his young life to this sacred cliff, to this myrrh-streaming Garden of the Panagia. The thoughts of flight, despair, faintheartedness and weakness which had assaulted him day by day departed and were replaced by a will to stay, by trust in God's providence, and by a strong and deep faith in Crucified Love. Delving into sacred letters elevated him into the spheres of high spirituality. He read in the *Ladder* of St

John that "Angels are a light for monks, and the monastic life is a light for all people" (Step 26:31), and his soul was filled with divine light. Furthermore, God Himself is light (1 John 1:5) and, as St Symeon the New Theologian (March 12 & October 12) says, "The things around God are light. The Father is Light, the Son is Light, and the Holy Spirit is Light (Gregory Nazianzen P.G. vol. 36, p.136). They are a simple light, light without mixture, timeless, before all ages, and which has the same honor and the same glory. Furthermore, whatever comes from them is light, because they are given to us from light. Life is light, the living water is light, love, peace, truth, the door which leads to the Kingdom of Heaven, and the Kingdom itself is light. Paradise is Light, the country of the meek, the crowns of eternal life, and the very garments of the Saints. Jesus Christ, the Savior and Deliverer of all is Light. The Bread of His immaculate Body is Light. The Cup of His precious Blood is Light. His face is Light. His hand, His finger, His mouth, His eyes are light. His voice is Light because it comes from light; the Comforter is Light. Hope and faith are Light" (Symeon the New Theologian, *Complete Works* Vol. 4, p. 59).

He derived much benefit from Elder Gabriel, as he himself admitted many times. He did not cease to say that Michael the Blind and Gabriel, his brother in the flesh, were his two guardian angels. The brilliantly shining beauty of their spiritual life dazzled him and he constantly looked for ways to imitate them. Finally, he made an important decision. On November 21, 1930, the Feast of the Entrance of the Theotokos, which their Kalyva celebrated as their patronal Feast, he was tonsured a monk by Elder Gabriel, and took the name Anthimos. Then his life completely changed. The dreadful promises he gave before God and men had to be kept with every sacrifice. Anthimos was a high-flying eagle, and he was drawn to the heights of spirituality. From then on he devoted himself to the practice of monastic life with greater zeal. He learned and lived the toil and the agony of ascesis, the order of spiritual exercise, the practice of unceasing prayer, the way of vigilance and wakefulness, the majesty of the liturgical and sacramental life. This day and night struggle did not make him yield. On the contrary, it made him strong. The words of St Athanasios the Great resounded in his progress-loving soul, "Let him who has comfort in this world not hope to receive eternal comfort. For the Kingdom of Heaven is not made up of those who are comforted here, but of those who are persecuted in this life in much affliction and distress" (Athanasios, *Concerning Virginity*, BEPES 33, p. 69). Of course, he tried to walk the aforesaid path of life with obedience, so that he might present his soul and his body to Christ free from the wounds of shame and of despondency, and receive the crowns of victory. He always kept vigil, and disregarded all pleasant things. He was not attached to anything earthly, not even if it seemed like genuine gold, not even if temporal enjoyments or opportunities for more comfortable residences presented themselves. He considered everything refuse, vapor (James 4:14), dust and ashes, murmuring to himself, "Vanity of vanities, all is vanity" (Eccl. 1:2).

He had his citizenship in heaven (Phil. 3:20) and he considered himself as a traveler hastening to the end of the path. He gazed beseechingly at the infiniteness of heaven and, as if he could see the Lord of Glory in his inner depths, he prayed, "Lord, remove me from the path of injustice and by Thy law have mercy on me" (Ps. 118/119: 29).

The young monk Anthimos unquestioningly obeyed his Spiritual Father, the virtuous Gabriel, whom the Ecumenical Patriarch himself had appointed as Spiritual Father of the Great Church of Constantinople. His words refreshed him like a heavenly dew and sweetened his inner being like a balsam. He listened to him reading with undiminished interest from Abba Dorotheos, "Not only must we all pay attention to what we are eating, but we must also abstain from every sin, so that while the belly fasts, in the same way the tongue should also fast. In other words, we must abstain from slander, from lying, from vain talking, from mocking others, from anger and, in a word, from every sin which we commit with the tongue. In the same way, our eyes must also fast and not look at vain sights. Let us not be haughty with words and not look at anyone with rudeness and audacity. In the same way, if we are fasting, our fasting is pleasing to God when the five gates of our senses are well closed and preserve us pure and undefiled". (Abba Dorotheos, *Homily On Fasting. Patristic Treasury*, p. 163).

Imitating the ancient ascetics, and having living examples of holiness in the Skete of his repentance, Anthimos disciplined himself in the implementation of God's will and the deadening of the passions. He admired the contemporary Saint Savvas the New (April 7), who reposed venerably at Kalymnos in 1948, and who had learned iconography in their Kalyva when he was a monk on the Holy Mountain. St Savvas of Kalymnos is the first one who depicted the figure of the miracle-working St Nektarios, with whom he was associated, and who was worthily made wondrous by the Lord for his pure life and exemplary behavior, whose body is preserved incorrupt. The quiet of the Garden of the Panagia, of the saint-nurturing Holy Mountain, and the grace of its supplier and protectress the Lady Theotokos, together with the prayers of his Elders, greatly helped Anthimos in the deadening of the "external senses" and in the activation of the "internal movements". As St Isaac the Syrian (Jan. 28) characteristically mentions, "Silence deadens the external senses and stirs up the internal movements."

Seeing his zeal for spiritual things, and also the purity of his heart, the discerning and wise Elder Gabriel put Anthimos forward for ordination to the priesthood. On April 13, 1933 Anthimos was ordained a Deacon at the Kyriakon of the Skete of St Anne, and to the priesthood on August 24, 1936 by the virtuous, charitable and humble Metropolitan Hierotheos of Militoupoleos, who practiced monasticism on the Holy Mountain. Suffice it to say that Hierotheos, who did very much for the ecclesiastical questions of Albania, once when he was going to Karyes gave his shoes to some poor ascetic and arrived at the capital of Athos with bare feet. The everp-memorable one was the true incarnation of holiness. He had completely hated money and was of those firm bones, from the leaven of those men who always held Orthodoxy high. He served in Asia Minor, Pontus and Korytsa. He always ran wherever they called him, and was a role model for everyone. He never forgot the high ordinances of the ancient Fathers of the nation and of the Church. The only estate he left was one chalice, which his heirs dedicated to the church of the Protaton, a carved icon, which was given to the Skete of St Anne, another one, which the blessed one destined for his successor Constantine and a little food, which was distributed to the indigent hermit monks.

Fr Anthimos received the office of Archimandrite, and later that of Spiritual Father, from Metropolitan Panteleimon I of Thessalonica, who was one of the monks in the neighboring Kalyva of St George of the Kartsonaion Brotherhood at St Anne's. The service took place in the chapel of the Metropolitan's residence in Thessalonica.

The vision which Fr Anthimos was granted to see at the time of his ordination to the diaconate is noteworthy. He saw the heavens opening and the church he was in without a roof. Earth and Heaven were united. The Church Militant and Triumphant rejoiced together at his ordination, which particularly pleased the Knower of hearts, the almighty Lord Jesus Christ. He was also granted to behold another vision after his ordination to presbyter. He saw all the priests who participated in the service bathed in divine light, except for one. Unfortunately, he was later defrocked, an event which the clairvoyant Elder had foreseen.

Thirst for Knowledge,
Longing for Virtue

Fr Anthimos approached the holy altar with the fear of God and elevating humility, and performed the Bloodless Sacrifice as a godly sacrificer and a priest who was an equal of the angels. He served the spiritual needs of his Kalyva, but at the same time fulfilled his monastic duties with exemplary strictness. As an "obedient child" (1 Peter 1:14), he tried to have his behavior conform to God's will, and his motto was, "Be holy, for I am Holy"(1 Peter 1:16).

For this reason also, he unquestioningly obeyed his Elders, who were experienced in the monastic life, and in the ways of fighting the good-hating demon. He had a longing to serve as a disciple, and accepted the counsels and the suggestions of the experienced monks, as a sponge soaks up water. This also was a sign of his humility, which was the foundation of his spiritual life. From this humility came his ceaseless contrition and his joy-bearing tears, which flowed from his very bright deeply blue eyes, were born. These tears led him to the purification of his soul and a more mystical knowledge of God's mysteries, as St Cyril of Philea in Thrace (December 2) says.

Hieromonk Anthimos thirsted for knowledge. In the beginning, for a certain time, he took refuge in the sacred Monastery of Xeropotamou to study its very substantial library. The books were his only treasure. The Holy Scripture, the God-bearing Fathers, the liturgical books and the sacred Rudder were his daily food. He knew whole passages by heart, which he unswervingly tried to implement in his life, or to rejoice in soul from memorizing them. Furthermore, he could precisely refer to the chapters and the verses of the texts of the Holy Scripture and of the Fathers. His unquenchable thirst for learning didn't stop there, however. He read systematically and deposited his knowledge in the treasury of his mind, from which he retrieved them at the appropriate moment, as if from the memory of a contemporary electric computer, to use them and make his godly-wise conclusions. The divine illumination which flooded him made up for the lack of "secular" education and made him literally wise. He moved in the area of every science with ease, so that even scholars who were specialists and professors remained astonished before the streaming and full speech of Elder Anthimos. He surprised everyone. It was not only theology which drew him. He was acquainted with philosophy, medicine, astronomy, mathematics, and history, since he had delved deeply into them. For this reason, when he was developing some topic which probably was not comprehensible to his audience, he used to say over and over again, "Did you understand me?".

Many said that Elder Anthimos, if he had remained in the world, would have been the greatest professor in Greece, and would have raised the knowledge and educational level of our universities. In addition to his theological erudition, at which one would wonder and would admire for its depths, he could speak with amazing ease about the Trojan War, the descent of the Dorians, the poisoning of Alexander the Great, the Galatians, the wars of Byzantium, but also about the beautiful Cretan songs, about Plato's ideas, about the Balkan wars, about the first man on the moon, and about all contemporary achievements. In general, he explained every subject about which those who took refuge in his humble Kalyva asked him so pleasantly and gracefully that he did not get tired, even if he spoke for hours. He spoke from the overflowing of his heart, and whatever he said was a distillation of divine wisdom and knowledge. Everyone on the Holy Mountain had trust in his knowledge and in his judgment and it is not by chance that Fr Paisios, that vessel of God's grace, once said to some pilgrim, "When Papa Anthimos speaks, keep notes. His words are wise, pure, full of divine grace."

In his teachings and counsels, Fr Anthimos always stressed the need to keep God's commandments. "This is the love of God, that we keep His commandments", he said repeatedly, "and His commandments are not burdensome," (1 John 5:3). Then he continued with the words of the godly-wise Kallistos and Ignatios Xanthopoulos, 'There is one path which leads to eternal life: keeping Christ's commandments. In these commandments are found every idea of virtue, particularly the three great ones, humility, love and mercy. Without these virtues no one can see the Lord' (*Philokalia* Vol. 4, page 269). We often heard him say, "Whoever loves God cannot but keep His commandments, and the heavenly Father will also love him for this. His grace will dwell in his heart, and will transform him into a living temple, according to the Evangelist John (John 14:23). So for me, keeping the commandments of God means that I have Christ in my heart, that I imitate His way of life on earth, and that I try to become a Christ-bearer, to ascend the Ladder of virtues which leads to unending blessedness."

Handicraft and Prayer

Like the ancient ascetics of the desert, Fr Anthimos had the unceasing prayer of the heart as his main work. He pursued his handicraft of iconography only to obtain necessities and to provide hospitality for his visitors. The pulses of his heart beat to the name of Jesus Christ and his pure lips ceaselessly repeated the prayer, "Our Lord Jesus Christ, have mercy on me". Through prayer he was united with God. Thus he avoided temptations and was protected from the influence of the devil, he cast away afflictions and everyday difficulties, he crushed despondency, lethargy and every earthly contact, and obtained the inviolable treasure of spiritual progress. Furthermore, with its brightly lit rays, his intellect was illumined and chased away every fog of pessimistic thought and despair. He did not forget that this is a spiritual mirror which reveals man's spiritual condition. The struggler Fr Anthimos considered sincere thanksgiving to God for all the good things He grants us, and supplication for the forgiveness of our innumerable sins with contrition and tears, to be a better way of prayer. He prayed simply, without cleverness, because many times, as he used to say, the stammering of infants moves the pity and the love of God the Father more than the carefully formulated prayers of adults. He did not say many things in his prayer, so that his intellect would not be scattered in seeking suitable words. He recalled that one word from the Publican propitiated God, and one word of faith saved the Thief. The words of the Apostle Paul, "I am the first of sinners" (1 Tim. 1:15) shook his being and, just as oil and salt make foods tasty, so his tears, which flowed and fell to the ground, also gave him wings. He spoke of soldiers and kings, and speaking in a charming way, said that just as a soldier shows his dedication to the king during a battle, a Christian also shows his love for God with correct and fervent prayer.

Fr Anthimos was a disciplined monk. All monks restrain their nature, one more and another less, but the Elder insisted, "The Kingdom of Heaven suffers violence and violent men seize it by force" (Matt. 11:12). The Kingdom of Heaven is gained by force and those who force themselves take it quickly and keep it tightly in their heart, so that it will not depart. He boldly confessed the definition of monasticism "the body works in order to be fed, and the soul is vigilant in order to inherit." For this reason, he also was exceptionally work-loving. Having in mind the saying "whoever wishes to become great among you, let him be the servant of all" (Matt. 20:26), he was first at all the services of his Kalyva. He was eager to fulfill every work, even the most toilsome and the most deprecating sort. He was the first in the garden, first in the kitchen, first in the iconography studio, where with abounding prayer he depicted the faces of our Lord, of the Most Holy Theotokos and of our Saints. He did all these things without ceasing to pray noetically for the whole world, both for the known and unknown, for illumination, an ascending journey and theosis.

Saving Obedience

Fr Anthimos, with his genuine and wholehearted obedience, prospered in God and achieved the divine promises. He knew that obedience is a great and wondrous virtue which strengthens the soul against the attacks of Satan. Our Lord Himself, Who "became obedient unto death, even to death on the cross" (Phil. 2:8) taught it to us. Paradise was closed when the first-created people abandoned obedience, and man is drowned in the abyss of misfortune when it is neglected today. Wherever obedience reigns, everyone is happy, virtue and holiness are cultivated and people become not only friends, but sons of God and ascend to the ancient glory from which they fell through disobedience. With obedience we deaden the members of our body upon the earth, the Elder often said, so that the members of the spirit may act better. Obedience is the tomb of our own will, from which the all-fragrant lily of humble-mindedness sprouts. Let us not forget that St Diadochos of Photike (March 29) stresses that obedience is the first among the preliminary virtues, since it abolishes haughtiness (that is, the great idea which one has about himself) and gives birth to humble-mindedness. For this reason to those who eagerly implement it, it becomes a gate which leads to the love of God. So let us implement it, if we wish to fight the devil, and this in its turn will infallibly show us the path which leads to every virtue. The Elder believed these things and unwaveringly implemented them in his life. For this reason he owed every honor and love to his Spiritual Fathers, and furthermore to the discerning, venerable, loving Gabriel. His honor toward them, he used to say, passes to Christ Himself and to the Holy Spirit, by Whom the gift of adoption (Gal. 4:5) is granted, and to the heavenly Father, from Whom every family in heaven and on earth is named (Eph. 3:15). As a deer hastens to the springs of water, so he hastened to his Spiritual Father to confess every sin and every thought to him, and to receive healing and forgiveness from him. He knew that the gift of "binding and loosening" was given to Spiritual Fathers, so that whatever they bind on earth is bound also in heaven, and whatever they loosen on earth will be loosened also in heaven (Matt. 18:18). Spiritual Fathers have received this grace from Christ, he used to say, and he obeyed them without question, without contradicting them, so as not to cause perdition to his soul and to lose the inheritance of the untainted goods and the unlimited joy and gladness. He often read in the *"Ladder"* (Step 4:23,24) of the obedience shown by the young monk Isidore to the presiding monk of his monastery, and who with his excellent words attained measures of virtue difficult to see, and gained the Kingdom of Heaven: "As iron submits to the will of the blacksmith, receiving a useful form from him, so I also submit to your will, precious Father, that you might make me a useful vessel of the gifts of the Holy Spirit".

Later on, when the same Elder became a famous Spiritual Father and they asked him about obedience he would say, "Obedience lifts us up to heaven, because it casts off the disobedience of the first-created people. It casts off haughtiness, self-satisfaction and likens us to God. Let us struggle to ascend to the likeness, because like is united with like. Let us unite with the Source of light, of virtue and of goodness, Who is Jesus Christ Himself."

Concerning the detailed confession of thoughts to a Spiritual Father, Fr Anthimos would add, "If we don't confess our thoughts, they will become snakes and beasts, and will devour us. The farmer who found a frozen snake and put it on his chest was unfortunate, because as soon as it warmed up, it cast off its sleep and bit him. Therefore, if we don't confess our thoughts, they will become works, and 'sin when it is fully formed brings forth death,' says the Apostle James (James 1:15). When we became monks, we promised to relate the hidden things of our hearts. Let us not forget that whoever was baptized with John's baptism confessed their sins. St Mary of Egypt (April 1) was a great sinner, but she repented so much that Abba Zosimas saw her walking upon the Jordan. We are obliged to preserve the promises of the angelic schema and to perform our monastic duties wherever we are. Every instance of negligence, whether voluntary or involuntary, must be confessed to the Spiritual Father, so that balsam can be applied to the wounds of despondency and for us to advance on the path of virtue, which reaches eternity. Speaking on the soul-saving topic of obedience the Elder always finished by saying, "If you have an Elder, you have God."'

The Repose of his Elder

If the all-perfect, almighty and all-controlling God, Who received human flesh, showed every obedience to Joseph and His Mother, and was subject to them, as the divinely-speaking Luke writes (Luke 2:51), but also fully submitted to His creature, then shouldn't I, the passionate and worthless one, the least of all people, obey my Elder, the most unerring director of my soul and my guide toward completion in Christ? The blessed Fr Anthimos would ponder these things and his eyes would tear up. He truly loved his Elder and served him humbly until his repose. Fr Anthimos describes the day when he left for eternity, August 20, 1959, as the bitterest day of his life. He had never wept so much as he did for his beloved Spiritual Father. During his childhood years he knew what it was to be an orphan, and had wept very much. Now he was crying at the temporal separation from the most precious person he had on this earth. Yes, he firmly believed that his Elder had pleased God, but the human pain melted his inner being. In a series of sketches which he himself painted, he shows descriptively the magnitude of his pain of soul at the departure of his Elder. It was four in the morning when Fr Gabriel fell and called for help with sobs crying, 'Anthimos, Anthimos!'

Struck with fear, he ran and saw his Elder on the ground, plaintively crying. Quickly, he bent over him and took him on his back in order to carry him to the Kalyva, while he constantly cried, 'My Panagia, help me!'

Elder Gabriel, however, breathed his last breath and his soul was transplanted in the fields of glory, in a place of green pasture, in a place of comfort. As Fr Anthimos wrote himself, the day of his Elder's funeral was 'my great drama and the unending flow of my tears.' At the time of his burial, unable to restrain himself, he fell over the relics of his Elder and cried out wailing, 'My Elder, my Elder, intercede now from on high with our Lord or me, your unworthy disciple!'

Here Fr Anthimos's purity of intellect should be stressed. God permitted him to see the departure of his Elder's blessed soul, and its ascent to the heavenly habitations, accompanied by a multitude of holy angels. At that same moment, Hieromonk Seraphim of the Kalyva of the Voliotes saw Elder Gabriel's soul being transported to heaven in a golden chariot.

A Way of Life
Equal to the Angels

Elder Anthimos seemed to everyone like an angel in the flesh. His face was full of grace, his gaze joyous. His deep blue sparkling eyes revealed the purity of his soul. Furthermore, "the eye is the light of the body" (Matt. 6:22). If it is sound, then man's whole body will be full of light, and the soul will be illumined and sparkle with holiness. He was simple and content with a little in his daily life. His personal belongings consisted of one set of vestments, not of the luxurious sort, sewn with gold thread, and a pectoral cross from Jerusalem, like those which parents hang on the beds of their children. He loved non-acquisitiveness and lived it according to the promise which he had made during his monastic tonsure. In his cell he had a sack filled with straw as his mattress, and a few small pieces of cheap furniture. Everything was necessary, and there was nothing superfluous. He had a measure and rhythm in his life. He regarded every day as his last and mourned and wept because he had not managed to make even a beginning of repentance, as he used to say. Even if he had been reconciled with the Archangel Michael from his adolescent years, when he first met the Elder Michael the Blind and would go up for Confession and to receive counsel at the hermitage of the Archangels at Vyrona, nevertheless he feared the moment when the Archangel would take his soul, to present it at the throne of the majesty of the three-sunned Godhead. The thought of the departure of the immortal soul from the mortal body always possessed him. Therefore, he prepared every day of his life and considered it as his last one. This thought, of course, did not lessen his diligence nor the output of his work. We must prepare as if we are dying now, he would say, and work as though we will never die.

Elder Anthimos always remained without wrath and was guileless like the little children, detached, though sometimes he pretended to be angry and irate. He did this in order to discourage those who spoke of his holiness with admiration, for he wished to avoid the arrogance which human praise causes to struggling souls. He was longsuffering and was not bothered by the unsuitable and improper behavior of his fellow ascetics at the Skete, nor of the indiscreet pilgrims. On the contrary, we always remember him as discerning, chaste, unchanging in his God-loving opinion, praying, humble, diligent.

He could not comprehend monastic life and spiritual resurrection without ever-flowing streams of love for every creature. Love is a very great thing, he would say. It is Christ Himself! He loved us to the point of sacrificing Himself for us. Let us also love one another with sacrificial love. Such a love requires violence, as the Gospel says about the Kingdom of Heaven, that "the violent take it by force" (Matt. 11:12). The beginning of our way to God must be "ever to force (or drive) oneself".

The Elder paid attention to two things more than all the others, which he also considered most necessary for cenobitic life, and also for living together as a family: obedience and humility, which proceed from the heart and alter man's old disposition.

The long drawn-out sacred services were Fr Anthimos's great and unspeakable joy. His behavior at them was similar to that of the courtiers and the guards before the Great King. Out of respect, he stood while chanting, even until his old age. When he was not liturgizing, he shone like a brilliantly luminous angel. He lived the Mystery of the divine Eucharist, and his hands trembled during the consecration of the precious Gifts. He would say, "I, the unworthy one, am dividing the living Lamb of God, Who is divided but not disunited, Who is eaten but never consumed". The divine fire touched him during the consecration. So, after every Divine Liturgy he would come out of church worn out and transfigured by the grace of the All-Holy Spirit Who aids in the good transformation of us all. For Fr Anthimos, the hours, the unending hours of the divine services, were times of sweet sojourning in Paradise. He kept company with the saints who were being celebrated, and he chanted their services. He conversed with them as a friend speaks with his friend, and gazed with longing at the future good things "which eye has not seen and ear has not heard, and have not entered into the heart of man, which God has prepared for those who love Him" (1 Cor. 2:9). Thus it can be explained why, until the last day of his life on earth, he asked that they chant the service of the saint of the day for him. The blessed one had placed the electrical cord of his life into the plug of eternity and had ceaseless communication with the Church Triumphant. Irresistibly drawn by the burning yet unconsumed bush of his heart, and with fiery faith he ceaselessly gazed at the transcendent ideal. He preferred to contort the structure of his bones with prostrations and petitions all night long in the stall of his chapel of the Entrance of the Theotokos and of the Kyriakon of the Skete of St Anne, and to be exhausted by the drawn out prayers and the many fasts of long duration, in order to obtain the uttermost of longings and to see the Lord with his own eyes, and not "through a glass darkly" (1 Cor. 13:12) as on this earth.

For Fr Anthimos everything around him was refuse. He had one goal: to win Christ, as the heavenly Apostle Paul wisely mentions (Phil. 3:8). He did not forget that he had come to the Holy Mountain unknown, a foreigner and a passerby intending to go across to the opposite shore of divine light, to go from death to life quietly, piously, humbly alone and unknown, and to be granted to live eternally after his natural death.

The Elder's Love for
the All-Holy Virgin

The Elder fostered a particular respect for the Most Holy Theotokos, in whose Garden he wished to spend his temporal life. The three-year-old "heifer" (Gen. 15:9, Heb. 9:13) whom her parents Joachim and Anna brought to the Temple, and who was placed in the Holy of Holies to be fed by the holy Angels, was his refuge in the difficult moments of his life. While celebrating and honoring the Entrance of the Theotokos, to which the church of his Kalyva was dedicated, at the same time Fr Anthimos celebrated his Exodus from the world of vanity and corruption. He did not forget that he been tonsured a monk on the day of their patronal feast and had changed his secular name and disposition for a monastic and heavenly one. For Fr Anthimos, as for every Athonite, the Most Holy Theotokos was Quick to Hear, the Sweet-kissing Mother, the Directress, the Hope of the Hopeless, the Consolation, the Fearful Protection, his own, his very own Refuge and Protection[1]. His soul overflowed with internal rejoicing, and tears of joy inundated his eyes when he chanted, "It is truly meet to bless you, the Theotokos...." On the day of his Kalyva's patronal Feast, the Elder felt a paschal joy and elation. The Synaxis of the Fathers of the Skete, the all night service with the beautifully singing chanters, and the very melodious and harmonious slow parts brought him to compunction, and gave him the most intense spiritual elation of the year. We could say that for Fr Anthimos, the spiritual cycle of the year began and ended with the Feast of the Entrance of the Theotokos. He said that he always spoke her name with reverence, since because of her virtue and humility she was granted to receive all the gifts of the All-Holy Spirit. Therefore, God also chose her, the only one among women, to be the Mother of the one Who is "without a mother in heaven" and "without a father on earth", His only begotten Son, our Lord, God and Savior Jesus Christ. She who dawned the all-bright Sun of Righteousness, also dawns the light of salvation in our hearts. She loosened the ancient curse, and as the new Eve opened the gates of Paradise with her divine-human Offspring, so that we, who were deprived of the delight of the Tree of Life because of the disobedience of our forefathers, might enter in. Thus people must glorify

---

[1] These are all names of wonderworking icons of the Mother of God on Mount Athos (Ed.)

night and day our All-Holy Virgin as the cause of everlasting joy and unending life, "who gave birth to the cause of gladness", as we state so beautifully in her Supplicatory Canon.

Once, when they asked him about the special reverence which he showed for our All-Holy Virgin, Elder Anthimos did not hesitate to open the scroll of his soul and to explain the particular reasons for his love for the blessed person of the Queen of Heaven saying, 'What can we give back to Her who is above all Creation?' After God, the Most Holy Theotokos surpasses every creature; and the Holy Scriptures, both the Old and New Testament, attest to her superiority. It is mentioned in Genesis. The first-created people disbelieved God and believed our Enemy, the devil. God told the serpent that he would be accursed, and that He would place enmity between him and the woman, between the seed of the serpent and the seed of the woman, that the seed of the woman would crush the head of the serpent under His heel (Genesis 3:16). So, what woman gave birth without seed? Since a woman does not have seed, the Lady Theotokos is the only woman who surpassed human nature and gave birth to the God-man. From the beginning, God declared that she would crush the head of the devil through the unutterable and seedless birth of our Lord Jesus Christ. The role of the Theotokos and her contribution to the salvation of the race of men is very clearly specified. The descendant of the new Eve, the new Adam of grace, the God-man Jesus, will definitively crush the ancient Enemy of man, the devil, and will again open Paradise for the exiles. What can we earthly creatures offer in return for this benefaction of the Theotokos to the whole human race?

"The Lady Theotokos not only deified us, but also protects us every day and frees us from every danger, especially today when we are exposed to so many dangers. The only thing we can offer is our ceaseless hymn and glorification for her favor. This hymn, of course, is always accompanied by fervent supplication that she will unceasingly protect us and guard us, since as a human being she knows human problems and weaknesses. She aids us on the Holy Mountain who have her as a provider and a refuge, guiding us toward perfection and theosis. The Panagia made promises to St Peter the Athonite (June 12), as St Gregory Palamas writes concerning this: 'I have chosen this Mountain, out of all the places on earth, to become a proper habitation for monks. Henceforth, it will be called the Holy Mountain. Whoever dwells here and wants to struggle against the common Enemy of man, the devil, will have me as an ally in their good struggle. I will become their invincible helper. I will teach them the things they must do, and I will indicate to them what they must avoid doing. I will be for them a provider, a physician and a nourisher. I will strive both for the feeding and health of their bodies, and also for the feeding and health of their souls. I will never let them fall from goodness and virtue. I will do these things as long as they live. After their death, I will ask my Son and God to grant full remission of sins to those who lived and reposed in repentance, and to number them among His Saints.'

"The Panagia also made a promise to St Athanasios the Athonite (July 5), when she appeared to him face to face. At that time the Saint was going to ask for the Emperor's support for his Lavra, and she told him to turn back. The

Saint, fearing the snares of the enemy, didn't pay attention. In order to convince him, the Panagia told him to strike the rock which was in front of him in the name of Him Who was born of her, and immediately after he struck the dry and arid rock it gushed forth a river of water, which flows to this day as a confirmation for everyone. St Athanasios was convinced that the Theotokos did not want him to go to the Queen of Cities (Constantinople), and so he turned back. Another time, when he was building the Very Great Lavra and he saw that his storage rooms were empty, he prayed to the Lady Theotokos and she filled them so much that the goods overflowed and poured onto the ground. Then the Panagia appeared to Athanasios and asked him, 'Do you still disbelieve?'

"Do you see how the Saints guarded themselves, so that they would not fall into the snares of the devil, who uses many crafts and even performs miracles, in order to deceive the people of God?

"Subsequently, the Panagia appeared to St Gabriel of Iveron (May 13, July 12), when her Icon the "Keeper of the Portal" came here. It has never left the Holy Mountain. Both it, and its various copies were made quite miraculous by her grace. In Russia the copies of the "Keeper of the Portal" performed many wonders. When the paralyzed daughter of the Tsar learned that her parents went to welcome her Icon, she got up and went on her own to the Kremlin where the sacred procession was. The Tsar was quite moved when he saw this miraculous event, and he gave all the land from the place where the miracle occurred up to the Kremlin to the Iveron Monastery.

"Then the Panagia appeared to St Gerontios (July 26), the abbot of the Bouleutirion Monastery, which was the first Skete of St Anne. It was near the shore, and was destroyed by the Catalan Spaniards in 1302. In its place today is the cell of St Eleutherios. Because that place was unsafe, St Gerontios went up higher, where he practiced hesychasm with another brother. He lived with much hardship, for that place was without water. The Panagia answered his prayer and brought forth water for drinking from the hard rock. The Saint's disciple, however, began cultivating a garden with greens, disobeying the command of the Theotokos.

"Therefore, the spring dried up and the Saint was much grieved. When he prayed again the Panagia appeared and told him, 'I gave you water for drinking and not in order to cultivate a garden, which distracts the mind of a monk who seeks stillness.'

"Nevertheless, with her blessing, water for their needs poured forth once more farther down from the saint's hermitage. The water which poured forth a second time is preserved to this day and is considered a holy water spring. It is a holy water spring of our All-Holy Virgin Mary and St Gerontios. The water is three inches deep. If you take all of it, it will remain three inches deep. At its mouth it is like steam. It doesn't have the heaviness of water. If you water plants with it they immediately dry up.

"Then the Theotokos and Queen of all appeared to a spiritual child of St Gerontios, to St Maximos Kausokalyvites (January 13) whom she supported. The other monks considered him crazy because he used to burn his huts. The Panagia appeared to him and said, 'Receive the grace against demons, and live at the foot of Athos. It is the will of my Son that you ascend to the height of virtues and become a teacher and guide to many in order to save them. Then heavenly bread was given to him to eat, because he was without food for quite a few days. As soon as he put it in his mouth, divine light surrounded him from above and he heard an angelic hymn. Thus the Theotokos ascended to the heavens. However, so much brilliance and fragrance remained at the peak of the mountain that the saint remained ecstatic, and did not want to come down from there, nor to be deprived of the heavenly fragrance and brilliance. After three days, at the command of the Theotokos, he went down to her church which is named "Panagia." There he lived for a few days and again ascended to the peak and venerated the place where the Panagia stood and he asked with tears that she appear to him again. However, he saw only light and smelled an ineffable fragrance, just as before, and his soul was filled with joy and gladness.

"The Mother of God has appeared to many holy ascetics and has consoled others. Some she helped, some she healed, and fulfilled the requests of others. Finally, she appeared to some brother who was carrying burdens on his shoulders. The work was very hard, and the road led uphill. The Panagia asked him, 'Why do you fret? Those who struggle for Christ's love not only have a great reward, but even their sweat will be considered as the blood of martyrs on the Day of Judgment.'

"Do you see how many promises we have? The Panagia intercedes for the whole race of Christians every day and helps everyone who calls upon her. She is the Ladder which people ascend and the Bridge on which God descends toward us. She mediates for us, protects us, and satisfies our legitimate requests. What more do we want?"

A Vessel of the Paraclete

What X-rays do for the medical profession, revealing what cannot be distinguished by the naked eye, the clairvoyant and prescient Elder also did for visitors. He had the power to discern the thoughts and the movements of the heart, the power to foretell future things, and to reveal the innermost depths of the heart. God bestowed this gift on him because of his pure way of life and his drive to gain the heavenly Kingdom. The Lord gave him a sense which is "above the senses." To many pilgrims he would foretell and foresee things which concerned them and particularly bothered them. He had a searching gaze, penetrating and simultaneously joyous and calm.

The gift of clairvoyance, which makes the God-loving soul "overseeing," is a gift of the Holy Spirit. Clairvoyance is born from discernment and is a fruit of humility and purity. Before his fall, the first-created man was clairvoyant by nature, but the overseeing power of his soul, which came from his purity, was covered as with a thick darkness due to the prevalence of the passions. With his life of childhood in Christ, the grace of God comes and opens the eyes of the soul which the devil had blinded, and immediately man begins to see things naturally. Thus, whoever has this spiritual vision has the capability of knowing the soul and the spiritual condition of each man and ascertaining, just by looking at him, if and how much he is granted to commune with the Holy Spirit. Clairvoyance is not related to the physical senses, nor is it a result of some psychosomatic alteration of man, but a return to the ancient beauty, as St Isaac the Syrian notes.

Elder Anthimos, who considered his clairvoyant gift to be a completely natural spiritual function, often repeated the words of St Anthony the Great (January 17), the prominent clairvoyant monastic saint of the desert of the Thebaid, "the intellect sees everything, including heavenly things, and nothing darkens it but sin. To the pure intellect nothing is incomprehensible" (Anthony The Great *Philokalia Vol 1*, paragraph 106). He also said, "A soul which is purified in all its parts and stands according to nature, is able to see more and farther than the demons, since it has become clairvoyant," (Anthony the Great BEPES 33, 24). With these words the holy Elder wished to stress that each one who lives and struggles against sin can have divine illumination and to see with the eyes of the soul whatever the eyes of the body do not see. This also was a sign of the Elder's humble-mindedness, for which he was also adorned by God with the gift of clairvoyance, which he wisely utilized to give appropriate counsels to whoever approached him and had a particular need.

A Strict Keeper of the Rudder

The Elder's character was marked by a precise observance of the sacred Canons of the Faith. Orthodoxy was more sacred than anything he had in the world. He had received powerful lessons from his strict Elder Gabriel, who blessed him to keep them unswervingly all his life. Thus the sacred Canons became his traffic lights, beacons lit by the divine fire, which transferred to him the messages of salvation, his bright lighthouses in the storm of his ceaseless ascesis, his compass for his unerring journey in through the murkiness of daily life. He always had the sacred Rudder near him, and he sought its counsel. He even knew the footnotes for every topic.

The Elder was always joyful, gentle, meek, sweet, but he was also strict in matters of faith, and would not make any adjustment, no economy, in matters of sin. On the subject of the union of the Churches, which for years has given rise to a lot of clamoring, Fr Anthimos would say:

"The Lord Himself assures us that 'the gates of Hades shall not prevail' against (the Church)' (Matt. 16:18). We Orthodox are the little flock which should not worry and be afraid that we are surrounded by a multitude of unbelievers, because our heavenly Father is pleased to give us the Kingdom of Heaven (Luke 12:32). Let the Pope rage with his millions; let the Protestants be rabid with their own things. They are all without God, as the Evangelist John writes in his second catholic Epistle, "Anyone who transgresses and does not abide in the doctrine of Christ, does not have God" (John 2:9). His ecclesiological understanding was also solid. Whenever he left the Holy Mountain, he would never perform the Blessing of Water, Unction services, or any other Mysteries without making a prostration before the local bishop. At first, he categorically refused to perform any Mysteries, until once at the Divine Liturgy at the hermitage of Vyrona he miraculously heard the Crucified Lord Himself saying to him from the Cross, "Anthimos, shepherd my sheep!"

From that time, as he often related, he decided to perform the Mysteries only for the edification of the believers and to offer counsel, for after the service he found the opportunity to address some consoling, comforting and edifying words to those present.

At other times, as the pious Mrs Helen Pappas related to us, that when she wanted to return to the old calendar, Fr Anthimos did not allow her to do so, and strictly scolded her saying, "You must go where your Church goes. On the one hand, we on the Holy Mountain follow the old calendar, but we are in spiritual communion with the official Church, and we are not inclined to split off from it. We might protest what is badly worded, but we are in the bosom of the Church, and we struggle to correct them from our place. Those who are outside the walls of the Church are exposed to the various wolves in sheep's clothing, who seek to tear them apart."

An Unerring Guide of Souls

The life of Elder Anthimos was a lifelong battle with the ancient Enemy, a constant contest in the arena of virtue and holiness on the path of action and vision. "He gave blood in order to receive spirit," as the God-bearing Fathers say. He lived not according to the flesh, but tried to harmonize his will with God's commandments, with the will of the Holy Spirit. His axiom was the voluntary crucifixion and

56

deadening of his own self, which was concerned with a secular mindset, material-loving pursuits, earthly cares and occupations. His ascetical struggles day and night served one goal: the life-giving deadening of his own self, the deliverance of his soul from the passions, and treasuring the various soul-nourishing virtues.

Elder Anthimos was distinguished by his humility. For this reason also the divine grace, which is a characteristic feature of the humble, had overshadowed him in every aspect of his life. The presence of Fr Anthimos gave forth an aroma of spiritual fragrance in Christ, since he was wholly "a sweet savor of Christ" (2 Cor. 2:15), which smelled fragrant and pleased everyone with the sweetness of his words. The joyfulness of his face manifested the internal alteration of his heart, which was "the change of the right hand of the Most High" (Ps. 76/77:10).

The Elder was a truly prominent spiritual man, in the more general sense of the term. He was firmly grounded in the faith of the Lord and in Orthodox traditions. He had placed elevating humility as a firm foundation for the edifice of his soul, and its roof was the dual love of God and neighbor. But in the narrower sense of the word, he was a Spiritual Father for multitudes of people, lay people and monks, who were comforted at his epitrachelion and received direction for the path of their life. For many years Elders who reached the measure of virtue on the Holy Mountain, such as Fr Ephraim of Katounakia, and Abbots of Cenobia, such as Elder George of Gregoriou, Elder Aimilianos of Simonopetra and Elder Alexios of Xenophontos, have called him "Spiritual Father." We have their written testimonies, and they regarded him as the preeminent Spiritual Father of Athos. Through his blessed little cell passed multitudes of people of every age and rank, the educated and the illiterate, whom he strengthened in soul. He regenerated many and showed them to be sons of light (John 12:36).

He received anyone who arrived at his humble Kalyva with love, and he bent over their problems with childlike innocence. He comforted all the wayfarers of life with kindness which he nurtured for everyone, the innocent and unselfish love he showed, and with his wise and practical examples. Like another Moses he guided the souls who had entrusted him with spiritual fatherhood from the Egypt of the passions to the noetic Promised Land of dispassion and "freedom in Christ." He knew that the work of the Spiritual Father is difficult. He had to achieve reconciliation, the reconciliation of the repentant sinner with the philanthropic and mercy-loving Lord. He had the Good Shepherd as a model, who came "to seek and save the lost" (Luke 19:10). For this reason he came seeking the deceived sheep with love, with tenderness, with self-denial, and many times with self-sacrifice. He agonized and prayed for the sheep who had gone astray, and he enlisted all the power of the boldness he had with the Lord to achieve the longed-for result, that is to guide the lost sheep back to the flock of the saved. Characteristic is this excerpt from a letter bearing the sacred seal of Elder Aimilianos, the Abbot of the Sacred Monastery of Simonos Petras to Fr Anthimos dated January 28, 1988. Among other things, the all-venerable erudite Abbot writes:

"We were moved by the eagerness and the swiftness with which you hastened for one soul which sought you. Of course, it is not only the value of one soul, which is worth more than all the treasures of the world, but it is also your own zeal and your immeasurable love, which grants you the agility of a small child, in order to serve your neighbor. Planted from flourishing youth in this Garden of the Lady Theotokos, and particularly in the Sacred Skete of her sanctified mother St Anne, you were watered by the living streams of genuine ascetical tradition of the Holy Mountain, you were robed in the priestly garment, you received the gift of spiritual Fatherhood, you united countless souls to the Lord, you comforted a multitude of disturbed consciences and, behold, even in honorable old age you carry on your blessed ministry by the grace of God."

The most venerable and erudite Elder George, Abbot of the holy, very populous Cenobium of Gregoriou, often addressed himself to Fr Anthimos on spiritual topics. In one of his letters which he addresses to him he seeks his help in a serious spiritual matter, as he mentions, "Given your great experience, your presence is very necessary."

Elder Anthimos in the hesychasterion of Vyrona did not hesitate to offer the laver of divine repentance to souls burdened and tired from sin. He longed to nourish weak souls with the bread of the Word of God, to free those enslaved in wickedness and iniquity with the key of absolution, and to restore them as communicants and co-inheritors of "the good things" (Matt. 25:34) which were promised from the foundation of the world.

The godly wisdom which the Elder had, and the clairvoyant gift with which he was adorned by God, were familiar to everyone on Athos and elsewhere. Many Spiritual Fathers, when they faced difficult conditions, sent the penitents to Fr Anthimos or urgently sought his opinion, which also counted for a lot. While there are very many cases when the cenobia sent prospective deacons and priests to the blessed Elder for a general Confession (covering their whole life) and a testimonial letter so that they might be ordained.

Fr Anthimos was particularly touched by the youth. His vast kindness and love, the meekness and simplicity of his heart had a beneficial influence on young souls and offered them the compass of salvation which showed them the true course to sail, so that they would not be wrecked on the treacherous shoals of sin. During the Mystery of Confession one felt a bond with the Elder, an identification, a union with the common electricity-bearing wire, which received current from heaven and imparted calmness, comfort of soul, rejoicing and happiness. Using his gifts, he first opened his heart to the penitent with his broad paternal smile, and when hearing the most grievous sins he replied calmly that he also was guilty of a similar sin, in order to approach the penitent by lowering himself and raising him up to repentance and purification. His simple questions were full of love and interest, and most importantly, the sinner felt the praying Elder as a mediator with the easily entreated Lord (Prayer at Vespers), from Whom he expected pardon, through his paternal mediation, and the power for a new light-bearing departure.

The Elder made the penitents' problems his own problems. He suffered with them, wept and tried to find edifying solutions, which would be in agreement with God's will. A few tears before the icon of Christ, he said, are the best medicine for healing the wounds of the soul. Christ is the physician who heals the wounds, and He is our excellent trainer.

The testimony of Kyriakos Michael, a student of theology from Kavala, is worth mentioning. In a 1996 letter, written after the Elder's repose, he mentions the following: "Elder Anthimos was my spiritual beacon and guide. He was a true Father of the Church, since he exercised his pastoral work with fervor of heart and clear discretion. He helped people who had some problem to identify it, and then advised them how to overcome it. He prayed day and night for people and for the solution of their problems.

He had endless forbearance and a spiritual charity for all his spiritual children, and also for everyone who visited him. Thousands of people came and visited him in his simple little cell. He taught everyone real love. His basic preaching was love for God. For more than sixty years he practiced asceticism. From his childhood until his deep old age he worked ceaselessly in the garden of his heart uprooting the tares of sin and planting the roses of dispassion. For this tireless ascesis the gift-giving Lord bestowed rich gifts upon him, like clairvoyance, foreknowledge, prophecy, and especially his miracle-working prayer. In combination with the gift of clairvoyance he also had the gift of spiritual healing, the power to restore health to sick souls of people and sometimes to their bodies as well. He provided this spiritual healing not only with his counseling words, but also by his silence and by his own presence. Elder Anthimos knew the details of both the time and of the place. It is unbelievable how much he saw, both things and people, and events which happened in the past, those which were happening in the present, and those which would occur in the future."

A pious pilgrim notes that his fundamental and great ascesis, apart from fasting, was constant vigilance and humility, and unceasing prayer. Every time I would meet Elder Anthimos I felt that my conversation with him was a spiritual feast. What impressed me greatly was the freedom he left to those with whom he conversed. I saw all the freedom of Orthodoxy incarnate in his face. He never obliged anyone to do anything whatsoever, and never indicated anything which took away the other person's freedom. Fr Anthimos was a man who did not make noise, but nevertheless drew people to himself. He did not say many things, he spoke a few measured words, and these were taken from the experience of his life. He spoke unpretentiously, simply, and won you over right away.

It is truly impossible for one to define the offering of someone like Fr Anthimos, a person who saw the world in the light and the love of God for everyone, a person full of hope despite his age, without problems, without anxieties and fears, a person who loved and humbled himself, thus giving an example for all of us to imitate.

Brilliant luminaries of the Holy Mountain used two descriptive titles of Elder Anthimos which are very near reality, and characteristic of his spiritual radiance. The monk Gerasimos of Little St Anne's, the venerable hymnographer of the Great Church of Christ called him God-bearing. He believed that the Elder's heart was a manger, which swaddled the divine Babe, the sweetest Emmanuel. Even though we all become "God-bearers" by approaching the Holy Mysteries and by receiving the Body and Blood of

Christ, this title, which the Church rarely applies to her children, is the most honorable one which was heard in reference to Elder Anthimos. The other venerable hesychast of our days, Fr Ephraim of Katounakia, called him wise. He was a living statue of God's wisdom, a torrent which gathered its waters from springs teeming with God. The faithful people of God who knew Elder Anthimos believed both things. The dear Father was both wise and God-bearing.

Dikaios of the Skete of Saint Anne

In the Sketes of the Holy Mountain, Dikaios is a title given to the one chosen to preside at the Skete after the elections every year on the eighth of May. His term lasts for one year, and he is concerned with the administrative and spiritual problems of the Skete. In particular, he assumes the expenses of offering hospitality to the pilgrims.

Elder Anthimos twice undertook the sacred task of the Dikaios and benefited many with his venerable personality, his words full of divine grace, his counsels, admonitions, his teachings and his indefatigable power to serve faithfully every pilgrim. Imitating our Lord Who was "girded with the towel" (John 13:5) of love, he prepared a meal to satisfy the hunger and quench the thirst, and to please everyone who approached. Admittedly, they had exerted great effort to get there on the inaccessible uphill footpaths of the Kyriakon of St Anne.

'We must give hospitality to one another without grudging' (1 Peter 4:9), he would tell the Fathers and his subordinates. If hospitality is the daughter of love, then Fr Anthimos, whose heart was full of love, had developed this virtue to the highest degree. He wanted to please every stranger, every pilgrim, to make him feel more agreeable, more pleasant. He always saw before him a soul for whom the Lord was crucified, an image of God. He saw the Lord Himself. As he used to say, "If you have seen your brother, you have seen your God."

With kindness he offered the traditional treat and the raki, which stops the sweat of the hiker and comforts him. Of course, strengthening coffee was absolutely necessary for whoever desired it. It was accompanied with a slice of Hagiorite bread or whatever fruit was in season. When he could, he always ate meals with those to whom he was offering hospitality, and conversed about every topic with them, sowing his spiritual seed with the always appropriate manner, which bore fruit most of the time. He acted as their tour guide in the Kyriakon of St Anne with eagerness and grace. He explained the beautiful frescoes and vividly recounted the lives of the ascetics depicted, and the figures of the martyrs. He spoke to them of the ancient icons of the Panagia, of St Anne and of other Saints, about the Bishop's throne, the votive offerings made of silver and gold, and the miracles which were hidden behind them. With great piety he would take out the holy relics for the believers to venerate. In a voice trembling with joy and emotion, he gave an account of the historic arrival there of the sacred relic of the foot of St Anne the Foremother of God. She is also the patron and the protectress of her Skete. When the time came for the pilgrim to depart he accompanied him outside, gave him his blessing and escorted him, bidding him farewell until he vanished at the end of the footpath. He wanted to pour even the last drop of his love into the pilgrim's heart. "Do not forget to entertain strangers" (Heb. 13:2), he repeated. "You don't know what this hospitality might produce! Abraham was found worthy to offer hospitality to the Holy Trinity Himself beneath the Oak of Mamre, and Lot to Angels before the destruction of Sodom" (Genesis Ch. 18-19). Furthermore, the Elder believed that hospitality to simple pilgrims returned to the person of Christ Himself, Who said, "Inasmuch as you have done it to one of these, the least of my brethren, you did to me" (Matt. 25:40). He wanted to compel everyone to love Him Whom he also served, and to whose orders and commands he was faithfully dedicated. John Karalis writes about Elder Anthimos in his book *It is shining on the holy mountain*:

"He was truly a living saint. He was a great figure, not only spiritual, but primarily human. His holiness adorns his worn-out face. Wisdom flows from his mouth, and love for his suffering fellow man pours forth."

He wrote this he after he tasted the good things of the hospitality of the unselfish worker of the Gospel, who knows to offer hospitality to strangers so that he does not become a stranger to God.

A certain pilgrim from Thasos was very moved and wrote, "I will not forget your hospitality, your kindness, your holiness and especially your utter humility. I will not forget that you washed my clothes. This is an exceptional mark of your humility as a figure of Christ."

Archbishop Christodoulos of Athens himself, who had visited him when he was the Metropolitan of Demetriados, wrote to him, "I turn my thoughts toward your sacred Kalyva, to offer profound thanks to you for the joy you gave us, receiving us with brotherly love, and for the many beneficial things which you discussed with us."

Mr Gregory Ziakas, current professor of the Theological School of the University of Thessalonica wrote, "Now that I have returned to the world again and pursued my life's struggle, I better understood how much those unforgettable days which I lived near you benefited me under your spiritual and also educational guidance. This time will constitute one of the most beautiful milestones in my life. I feel this even more now, therefore my gratitude for your real Christian love, whose beneficial influence I unstintingly received, will endure".

Pilgrimage to his Homeland

The Elder Anthimos always had the compass of his life turned to the noetic pole star of heaven. He tried to implement St Paul's saying: "forgetting what lies behind, while straining forward to what lies ahead" (Phil. 3:13), because he made it the goal of his life to receive "the reward of the high calling of God in Jesus Christ" (Phil. 3:14). He did not leave the Holy Mountain without a specific reason, and his movements were always measured. He forgot whatever happened in his past, which he had left behind him, and stretched out constantly and hastened to those things which were before him. He heard the voice of God through Jesus Christ calling him to receive the reward of eternal joy, the reward of the Kingdom of Heaven.

The Elder maintained some contacts with Kallianoi, the village where he was born. His brother Anastasios was living and, although Fr Anthimos considered the whole world as his brothers for whom he prayed daily, nevertheless the fraternal blood drew him and he wanted to visit him. His evil stepmother had already died, or rather committed suicide like Judas, unrepentant for her unruly life. She fell into the Asopo River and was drowned to seal her all-foul life with a dishonorable and blasphemous death. St Charalambos, his village church, where he was garbed with the robe of a Christian, always lived in his memory. Above all however, he wanted to visit the little monastery of St Paraskevi in the very green valley above the village. There his first cousin, the nun Kassiani (Katherine Zapheiropoulou in the world) lived in asceticism. This simple and unlettered hermitess of Kallianoi, who had been adorned by God with the gifts of the Holy Spirit, also attracted   the Hagiorite ascetic's attention. Both cousins had abundantly received the gift of foreknowledge from God because of the purity of their souls and bodies, and their communication was soul-profiting, strengthening and edifying.

The church of the monastery of the holy monastic martyr Paraskevi was built in 1888 through the initiative and personal work of Constantine Karakousi of Athanasios, as a relevant inscription informs us. He was led to this location after a dream and found the foundations of the old building and the sacred icon of St Paraskevi, which today is kept in the church. The foundress of the monastery was Kassiani, who lived there in asceticism from age of thirteen. She was a novice until 1925, when she received the angelic schema and her name was changed from Katherine to Kassiani. She was highly respected in her village, although "no prophet is accepted in his own homeland" (Luke 4:24). She reposed on February 1, 1986 at the age of 103, full of days and full of virtues. Furthermore, she had foreseen her end and had notified her nephew to prepare the necessities for the funeral.

Something noteworthy took place during the German occupation. When the conquerors were burning all the villages, the Kallianotes left for Zireia. However, having the Lord as her champion and St Paraskevi as her helper, Kassiani remained behind and continued her ascetical rule undisturbed. The Germans, in their effort to find out where the Kallianotes hid, went to the monastery and pressured Kassiani to reveal the hiding place of her fellow villagers. She, of course, imitating our heroic forebears, refused to speak, and for this reason they ordered that she be hanged. However, in a wondrous manner the handkerchief with which they went to hang her was cut, and they left trembling, because they saw a bright light surrounding her.

This hermitess was the pole star which drew Elder Anthimos to Kallianoi, and certainly he must be rejoicing with her now in the glory of the Three-Sunned Godhead. The Elder walked the narrow alleys of his village with youthful vigor. As he walked, his mind returned to his childhood years, which had not been so pleasant. Of course, the passing years had blurred his ugly recollections and had strengthened the few but beautiful memories of his dear beloved mother, of whom he had been so prematurely deprived. He thanked the Lord for everything, however. Above all because He granted him to step again on these blessed areas and to chant a Trisagion in memory of the one who brought him into the world, and whose face he could see only faintly in his memory.

The Elder's fellow villagers suggested that he become a priest in their village, since all of them were proud of his spiritual progress and erudition. He refused without hesitation.

"I lived here during the first twelve years of my life," he would say, "and all the rest which the Lord granted me on the Holy Mountain. So, I consider Athos as my earthly homeland and there I will remain for as much time as the good God allows me to live before He calls me to the heavenly homeland, the future city, for which we must all nurture particular nostalgia, like people living abroad who very fervently desire to return to their homeland."

He Spoke with his Silence

In 1990, on the birthday of our Church (Pentecost), the Elder decided to make a pilgrimage to the Great Church of Christ and the Ecumenical Patriarchate. He had been invited by the director of the private office of the Patriarchate, Metropolitan Bartholomew of Philadelphia, the current Ecumenical Patriarch, and by the Principal of the Theological School of Halki, Metropolitan Maximos (Repanelli) of Stavroupolis. Patriarch Demetrios received him at the Phanar with much love after introductions and notifications, as the most prominent charismatic Elder of Athos. He considered the Elder's visit there a particular blessing for the Ecumenical Throne. The Patriarch and Elder met for the first time, according to the former's desire, at the sacred altar of the Patriarchal Church of St George, next to the Holy Altar Table at the end of the Divine Liturgy. At an audience where the Patriarch later received him in his office, the following odd thing took place:

The meeting of the two men lasted about half an hour, but neither the Patriarch nor the Elder spoke. There seemed to be absolute silence. In reality, however, God spoke to them in their hearts, and they themselves spoke to one another in their hearts. The Elder who had been purified from passions, desires and his own will, had been filled with the grace of the Holy Spirit, the source of every truth. Through the invocation of Jesus Christ's name, which contains all names, he lowered his intellect into the secret area of the heart, to speak within his vast silence with God, the Good Shepherd, Who leads everyone to the pastures of salvation.

The silence was broken by the Elder's disciple, Hieromonk Cherubim. Troubled by the extended silence, he addressed the Patriarch saying, 'Your All-Holiness, our presence has tired you.' The Patriarch replied, 'No, on the contrary, the Elder's presence refreshes me!'

The communication of the two men was clearly spiritual, you see. Words were superfluous, for their souls had a common point of contact. They spoke through our Lord Himself.

Later, during the Elder's visit to Halki, Metropolitan Maximos, the head of the school, ordered Metropolitan Cyril of Seleucia to kneel down and feed the Elder with a fork "as a sign of piety," because the Elder had engulfed the famous saint-nurturing Queen of Cities with sanctity.

With the Border
Guards of Jerusalem

Elder Anthimos, like every Christian who has even a little reverence for divine things, longed and desired to visit and to see with his own eyes the lands which were sanctified by our Lord's feet. Aflame with this longing he entreated the All-good God and Father to let him visit the All-holy Tomb, the source of our resurrection, and all the wondrous and sacred shrines of Holy Zion, and all the surrounding area as far as the God-trodden Mount Sinai. There the Lord descended "in darkness and in a tempest, and with the sound of a trumpet" (Heb. 12:18-19), and handed the tablets of the Law to His servant Moses. The Lord heard the voice of his burning longing, and He granted his petition and filled his humble soul with joy and gladness. Shudders of emotion passed through him and waves of utmost emotion shook his inner being on his trip to Palestine, when he chanted with compunction, "Behold, we are going up to Jerusalem" (Matt. 20:18).

There were some Athonite monks in his group to the Holy Land, including Fr Barlaam, Fr Tryphon and others. It is important that the Elder had deeply appreciated the meaning of this visit. This was not just the Holy Land, it also was the Brotherhood of the Holy Sepulcher. The Holy Land sanctifies pilgrims with the grace of the incarnate Word of God. The Brotherhood of the Holy Sepulcher, the border guards of Orthodoxy, needs support. For centuries now, in the mouth of the wolf, with their feet and hands, they try to preserve the Hellenism of the sacred shrines. They live under harsh conditions, amid impiety, corruption and in dissolute surroundings, under the blasphemous eyes of the heretics and heterodox.

Like a honeybee interested only in honey and nectar, Elder Anthimos tried to gather from the various sacred shrines, and to store in his memory the most beautiful things he found, so that this visit might be edifying and soul-profiting. His visit to the Chozeba Monastery, where he was received by the charismatic abbot Elder Amphilochios, was moving. Fr Anthimos remained speechless, seeing him welcome him and hearing him call him by name. Tears filled his deep blue eyes when Fr Amphilochios offered him portions of the myrrh-flowing relics of the venerable Chozebite martyrs, the three thousand Fathers and Abbas who were martyred during the invasion of the Blemmyes in 614 A.D. These two charismatic Elders, each embracing the other, provided those present with extremely moving moments which cannot be easily repeated.

At the dreadful Golgotha, the Elder could not restrain his tears from flowing in streams from his eyes. Mentally he saw the Lord nailed to the Wood of the Cross with blood flowing from His immaculate hands and feet. He felt the breath coming heavily from His chest and heard His voice slowly whisper, "Forgive them, holy Father, for they know not what they do" (Luke 23:34).

On his knees he venerated the spot where the Wood of the Cross had been set up, and embracing it, he drenched it with the streams of his tears. You see, the crucified Love, the suffering Lord, always spoke in his heart. He "was crucified for us, in order to grant us remission of sins" he said, He "bears our sins and is pained for us" (Is. 53:4).

Joy mixed with emotion filled the Elder's soul, when he saw the All-holy, God-receiving tomb, which received the immaculate body of Jesus. The emotions which he felt at the site of the sacred Sepulcher of the All-holy Tomb cannot be described. From here the King of Kings and Lord of Lords, the Maker and Creator of creation arose. Here the myrrh-bearing women saw the burial clothes "lying apart" (John 20:7) and a radiant Angel asking them, "Why do you seek the living among the dead?" (Luke 24:5).

The building of the Holy Sepulcher is about eight meters in length, 5.55 meters wide, and 5.5 meters high. It was built by Greek hands, so that we can always remember the infallible words of our Lord, which He spoke when he saw some Greeks, "The hour has come for the Son of man to be glorified" (John 12:23).

Its front view is majestic and the whole edifice is girded round about by a troparion in the Greek language which is carved into the stone: "Let the nations and peoples praise Christ our God, Who voluntarily endured the Cross for us, and was three days in Hades. Let them worship His Resurrection from the dead, through which all the ends of the earth are illumined."

After he embraced the stone which the angel of the Lord rolled away from the All-holy Tomb, the Elder knelt and kissed it tenderly with his lips, and drenched it with tears from his eyes. At that moment he longed for his soul to be separated from his body, free to fly to the Sweetest Jesus Who "redeemed us from the curse of the Law by His precious blood" (*Priest's prayer at the Proskomedia*).

Reborn and strengthened by his pilgrimage to the Holy Land, the Elder returned to the Holy Mountain, to continue the Golgotha of his ascetic life, which would lead him to our resurrected Lord.

A Chronicle of one of the Elder's Days

Because death comes "as a thief in the night" (I Thess. 5:2), the Elder was always vigilant. 'A wakeful eye purifies the intellect,' he would say, and he fought for sleep not to overtake him. He would not allow his body to lie down, but he would place his hands on his head and pull it forward, so that he would not rest. He did not hate his body, which is a temple of God, but he hated sin and tried with the melting of his flesh to humble its uprisings. He filled the entire twenty-four hours with prayer and handiwork. He was a lover of the prayer of the heart, and it was never absent from his lips. He was also a lover of labor to the utmost degree; he worked ceaselessly in the iconography studio, in the garden, in the kitchen, in cleaning the Kalyva. In his cell he practiced prayer and contemplation. There in the dark, he tried to put into practice the things that he learned from the patristic books. Without fail, he made three hundred prostrations for himself and more prostrations for whoever asked him. He had an amazing familiarity with hymnography. He recited all the Kontakia of Compline from memory. His food was frugal. Even outside the HolyMountain, he never ate meat from the time of his tonsure until his death. When he confessed at the Kyriakon he ate whatever was at hand. He would be satiated by his offering to others, and by his kenosis. He did not skip anything in the services. Usually, he was both the Priest and the Chanter. He never neglected his Rule. Hospitality was a substitute for hours of handicraft, and was always accompanied by noetic prayer. The two facets of his daily life could be summarized in his effort to please "God and men." He was an earthly angel, and a heavenly man.

The Elder was very moved when he read the Life of St Seraphim of Sarov (January 2). A few days later, in a conversation with his disciples, he said, 'I have come to know all the struggles of St Seraphim, though not according to his own measure, of course. I did not come to know the cold at all. I can't endure that. May God forgive my weakness.'

Elder Anthimos was pure physically and in his soul. He was a virgin. Just as the Evangelist John was granted spiritual gifts because of his virginity, so Elder Anthimos also became a treasury of divine gifts. In return, God richly poured out upon him the gifts of foreknowledge, clairvoyance, and healing.

He Foretells his Death

Elder Anthimos fought the good fight and ascended the Ladder of virtues. What more could he expect in this life? The ramparts of heaven, where the clear sound of those who celebrate and ceaselessly cry out, "Glory to Thee, O Lord" awaited him. Like a bright star, Elder Anthimos traced a bright path in the spiritual firmament, and now he was ready to set so that he might dawn in eternity, where together with the Saints and the Angels, he will brighten the all-luminous heavenly arch, and will illuminate the Church Militant. The toil of spiritual and physical struggles and the burden of old age had already exhausted the tireless spiritual and indefatigable soldier of the faith. The "end has drawn near" (1 Peter 4:7), and he saw it. He prepared for his departure and foretold it to individuals, not only to those of his Brotherhood, but also to those beyond his narrow surroundings.

A year before his repose the Elder said to his disciple Fr Cherubim, 'A reason will be given, and I will become sick for a little while, then quickly depart. You will be here and will take care of me!'.

Mr George Tarasides, an agriculturalist from Panorama, Thessalonica, notes in a letter which he sent after the Elder's repose to his disciple Fr Cherubim (now Elder of his Kalyva):

"On June 18, 1996, a Tuesday, I wanted to telephone the Skete of St Anne to speak with Fr Basil of the

Brotherhood of the Voliotes, and called the telephone number of your own Brotherhood of the Theophileon by mistake. Of course, I did not realize it, and so I asked the person who answered for Fr Basil.

'You have made a mistake, my dear child,' the trembling elderly voice answered. 'You should dial 23320.'

'Oh! Fr Anthimos, is that you?' I continued.

'Yes, my dear child, it is I. Who are you?' he replied.

'Father, I am George Tarasides, the agriculturalist. I came this year on Holy Tuesday with my friends Dimitri and Constantine, and we asked you for your blessing. You gave it to us willingly, and we thank you.'

'I understand, my child. I remember you.'

'Now, Father, we will come on August 17th, to go up to the peak of the Holy Mountain to worship.Therefore, please permit us to visit you and receive your blessing again.'

'Well, you are welcome to come, my dear child, and you have my blessing from now. However, I will not be here in August, my dear child.'

'Why do you say this, Father? August is very near, and I am sure that we will speak face to face.'

'Well, my dear child, I am very old and tired. You will come, but I will not be here,' he repeated.

Only ten days later, events showed that our beloved Fr Anthimos, blessed by God, knew what he was saying."

Mr Constantine Kanellos, a teacher from Ithaca, also notes in his letter:

"I had the great blessing of becoming acquainted with Elder Anthimos on June 20, 1996, a Thursday, when I visited the Skete of St Anne just a few days before his venerable repose. I had heard, and also read that he was a choice and sanctified Spiritual Father, and I admit that I climbed the stairs for the blessed Kalyva of the Entrance of the Theotokos of the Brotherhood of the Theophileon with particular joy, and also sweet trepidation. Like thirsty deer, two youths from Athens also came up with me, and one was from Aridaia.

Upon arriving we sat in the yard, because some other pilgrims who arrived before us were speaking with Elder Anthimos. From the very green flat area we saw in the distance the Kyriakon of the Skete, its Kalyves, and in the background, the vastness of the sea. Soon, the venerable face of the Elder appeared, a very kindly, sweet, consoling, joyous face. We made a prostration and, being obedient, we went up to venerate the miraculous Icon of the Entrance of the Theotokos. We came down right after that, and then an unforgettable spiritual conversation with the blessed Elder followed. He awaited us full of the sweetest and disarming love, a spontaneous, lavish, ardent love for God's creature who was hurting.

His clear blue eyes look at us right in the eyes, wishing to enter the very depths of our tired souls. They were a sea of love, interest, paternal compassion and loving care. Simultaneously he patted our hair, he pulled our ears, he kept us close to him, and he counseled us with the experience and the discretion of his spiritual majesty.

Personally I felt great awkwardness and emotion seeing the aged venerable Elder hugging all of us with an unheard of love, overpowering, the love of Christ, so foreign to the secular times of unfriendliness and disbelief in which we live.

He especially rejoiced when I told him that I am from Ithaca. He was like a small child! He advised me to become very crafty, like Odysseus. The Elder's knowledge of ancient Greece impressed us. He found Hellenic characteristics in us, whereas at other times he stretched the skin over the veins of our hands so that we could see the Greek blood which flows in them. He also told us of his pilgrimage to the wonderworking St Gerasimos of Kephalonia (August 16 & October 20) which is near Ithaca, and about the possessed fellow who burst out shouting that a compatriot of St Gerasimos had come to venerate him. It should be noted that both St Gerasimos and Elder Anthimos were from the mountains of Corinthia.

Subsequently, he suggested that I study a particular Epistle of the Apostle Paul from the New Testament, and as the conversation approached its end he told me, 'I have fought the good fight, I have finished the course, I have kept the faith. Henceforth, the crown of righteousness is laid up for me' (2 Timothy 4:7-8).

I admit that these words made a particular impression on me, because they did not fit into the flow of the conversation we had with the Elder.

Upon leaving he gave us a little icon of the All-Holy Virgin Mary, and a small fragrant carnation from the pots in the yard, a symbol of a warm heart, which overflowed with the myrrh of humility, simplicity, and vast love.

As we came out, I stood at the end of the line and bade the Elder Anthimos farewell. Suffused with light, he stood in the middle of the yard and blessed us.

When I returned to Ithaca I enthusiastically told my Spiritual Father of my experience with the Elder of Love. Between seriousness and joking, I mentioned the Elder's last words from the Epistle to Timothy, thinking that perhaps the Elder was prophesying my death, and that this would be my last summer. I was dumbfounded, however, when I learned a few days later of the venerable repose of Fr Anthimos after a sudden accident in the vineyard of his Kalyva. The blessed Elder had foreseen his translation from temporal things to the eternal things.

His Venerable End

As a man the Elder was subject to death according to the decision which was announced to the first-created people because of the transgression of His command, "you are earth and unto earth you shall return" (Genesis 3:19) and because "it is appointed for people to die once, and after this, judgment." (Hebrews 9:27). Thus the time came for him to depart for the eternal homeland. During his last days he repeated joyfully to his disciples, "The time of my departure has come" (2 Timothy 4:6.) He awaited death in order to be united with his beloved Jesus. His death took place in the same manner as that of Elder Gabriel, his greatly mourned Spiritual Father.

At the vigil of the Ascension it seemed that Fr Anthimos did not have the strength to stand up which characterized him a long time ago. It was his last vigil at the Kyriakon of the Skete. Afterwards he limited himself to his cell doing all the services with his disciples. He did not skip anything until his last moment. He received strength from the Saints of each day whom he prayed would become mediators for him at the dread time of Judgment. On June 26, as he was trying to take care of the vineyard in the yard of his Kalyva, he fell and suffered many fractures. His disciples hastened to his entreaties and offered him first aid. He was transferred to his cell with great care, and immediately he asked to partake of the Immaculate Mysteries, in order to receive courage and strength. As pain was cutting off his breath, he opened his mouth to receive the Lord, and he shed tears when he heard Hieromonk Cherubim saying, "The servant of God Anthimos receives the Precious and All-Holy Body and Blood of our Lord God and Savior Jesus Christ, for the remission of his sins and unto life everlasting."

He was transferred to the military hospital of Thessalonica by helicopter, where his blessed soul was separated from his earthly flesh, like a sparrow breathing its last breath. Before surrendering his soul into the hands of the Living God, he gave his disciples his last counsels. He spoke to them about all the spiritual matters and the temptations they would face. To all he gave the appropriate medicine which would lead to the closing of the wounds of soul and final therapy. He lifted his eyes to heaven, like our Lord on the Cross, and slowly mumbled, 'Into Thy hands, O Lord, I commend my spirit' (Luke 23:46).

A smile was on his lips. He looked around at everyone with vast love and closed his blue eyes, to open them in the festive atmosphere of the Kingdom of Heaven.

The Dikaios of the Skete, Hieromonk Seraphim, the disciple of Hieromonk Cherubim and also his disciple Monk Theophilos, described the accident in the investigative clergy report. We reprint Hieromonk Seraphim's text which says:

"On June 26, 1996, around 10:30 worldly time, I learned that Fr Anthimos, the Spiritual Father, had been stricken. During the afternoon of the same day, specifically about one o'clock, I went to visit him in his Kalyva of the Entrance of the Theotokos. When I went, I saw the Elder was conscious, but he could not move, because his spinal cord was injured. I asked him immediately how he had been hurt, and Fr Anthimos told me that he himself was responsible for his injury, and no one else. He told me that in the morning and while he was in the yard of his Kalyva, he tried to tie a vine branch, to help it climb up from the garden where it was planted. However, he lost his balance in his effort, which resulted in him falling from his yard to the garden and getting hurt. There is a difference of about 2.5 meters between the height of the yard of the house and the garden. The next day, because Fr Anthimos's health worsened, he was transferred by helicopter to 424 G.S.N. in Thessalonica. On June 28, 1996 I learned that he had reposed. The Elder Papa Anthimos, in the world Constantine Zapheiropoulos, was an eminent personality of our sacred Skete of St Anne, an important man and Spiritual Father, and his death is a great loss for the Skete of St Anne, for the Holy Mountain and our Church in general. Until the moment of his fatal wound, he was my Spiritual Father."

The Elder Anthimos's bier was transferred to the Holy Mountain, where the news of his death spread like lightning, and filled all the Athonites with very deep grief. Just as we see in the icon depicting the repose of St Ephraim the Syrian all the hermits coming from every corner of the earth to accompany the Saint to his last dwelling, so we also saw the Hagiorite monks together with the friends of the Holy Mountain who were of the laity hastening to the Skete of St Anne to receive the blessing of the aged Elder for the last time, and to unite their prayers for the repose of his very pure soul. The Fathers transferred the sacred bier in their hands from the dock to the Skete taking turns in the uphill footpath, not so much because of the difficulty of the ascent as to permit everyone to receive a blessing from the blessed Elder. His funeral service was chanted at the Kyriakon of St Anne, and according to his desire, it was not elaborate. The Elder, who had been simple in all his life, also wanted his funeral service to be simple. Only the Fathers from his Skete of St Anne, Fathers from the surrounding Sketes, such as New Skete, Katounakia, Little St Anne's, representatives of the Cenobia of the Holy Mountain, his spiritual children and lay people from every corner of Greece, who arrived on Athos on their own initiative to pay respects to the blessed Elder and to receive his blessing for the continuation of their very difficult struggle. Also attending were representatives of the Fathers from the ruling Monastery, the Very Great Lavra. The burial took place at the nearby cemetery of the Skete according to the custom of the Holy Mountain.

The forty day memorial, on the contrary, took place with much formality. Metropolitan Christodoulos of Demetriados (now Archbishop of Athens), and the neighboring Metropolitan Nikodemos of Ierisssos and the Holy Mountain attended. Also Professor George Martselos, the Political Administrator of the Holy Mountain, who after the Hierarchs, also praised the Elder's virtue, his gifts and his contribution to Hagioritic monasticism. Furthermore, at his suggestion, the Civil Administration of the Holy Mountain covered the greater part of the expenses for the Elder's funeral service and memorial.

He Pleased God

Angels received the soul of the reposed Elder and transferred it to the throne of God's Majesty. There is no doubt that Fr Anthimos received the reward of the high calling of God in Jesus Christ (Philippians 3:14) which he sought with longing during his whole life. We have three testimonies from people that his tomb was fragrant. They sought the fulfillment of their petitions, calling upon the Elder's boldness before the Lord, and received the fragrance as an answer.

There was a married priest of Athens who was associated with the Elder, and after his repose asked that they give him a piece of his priestly vestment as a blessing. He received an epimanikon (cuff), and with it he healed a sick person who had become gravely ill. Also, a young possessed person was healed and calmed down when Fr Theophilos, the Elder's disciple, read the Elder's Troparion. Surprised, those present heard him say, "You have saved me, Anthimos!".

Eulogy

This speech was delivered by the Elder's disciple, Archimandrite Cherubim Apostolou, at his fortieth day memorial service, and was published in the September-October volume of the magazine "Protaton." It is reprinted here:

"If we believe that Jesus died and rose again, so also, through Jesus, God will bring with him those who have fallen asleep (I Thessalonians 4:14).

What, specifically, has gathered all of us here today, Your Eminences, holy Hierarchs, and my venerable Fathers and brethren in Christ? The special thing is the forty day Memorial of the Holy Elder Anthimos the Hieromonk, the Spiritual Father. Who called us here? The Holy Elder, called to the throne of God, has called us here. Why did he call us? To hymn the name of the All-Holy God, to glorify His grace, to give thanks for all that He richly grants us, and to offer a prayer entreating forgiveness and mercy for the soul of the "blessedly reposed" Elder. The Monastic Saints who are with Christ received the most venerable one from us, and he who was with us forty days ago was transported from us.

He who occupied himself well with God was translated from us.

The unselfish, unerring teacher, who was strong in faith and brave in his disposition, was translated from us.

The irreproachable, brother-loving one, who was all things to all people, was translated from us.

The long suffering, patient one who did not love glory, he who was pure in soul and body was translated from us.

The faster, who settled for a few things, the labor-loving one was translated.

The perfect monk and disciple was translated.

The excellent liturgist of the Most High, the very experienced Spiritual Father was translated.

The guileless and innocent iconographer was translated.

The guide of many Elders, Hieromonks, Monks, and thousands of souls was translated.

The man of prayer, the man of love, the man of humility, the man of God was translated.

The flower of St Anne's, the boast of the Holy Mountain, the Hagiorite figure of Orthodoxy was translated.

The virtuous and holy man was translated, who from the age of seventeen loved God and people with his whole soul.

He left us orphans and departed to our eternal homeland.

He left corruption and ascended toward incorruption.

He set from the world and has dawned in heaven.

He left the vain life of the world and dwelt in the Jerusalem on high.

He left the vanity of life and came to the blessedness above.

He left vain perplexities and advanced to peaceful places.

He came out of the winter and the storm of the world and arrived at a calm port.

He left the vain shadow of this world and ran to Christ, the Sun of Righteousness.

We his disciples did not remain orphaned. On the contrary, we glorify the Triune God and the patron and protectress of our sacred place, the most blessed Theotokos, for she granted us her pastoral care of such a virtuous man of God in all things. He was honorable and experienced in spiritual matters, in action and vision. We lived, by the grace of God, sitting at his feet for sixteen continuous years. Full of divine counsels, ascetical efforts, temptations, spiritual contests, of joy, sadness, pain and tears. Many times we felt that it became impossible for us to escape the snares and the plots of the ruler of the world of this age. Then we remembered the Apostle Paul's saying, "Who shall separate us from the love of Christ? Shall tribulation, or distress, or persecution, or famine, or nakedness, or peril, or sword? As it is written, For Thy sake we are killed all day long; we are regarded as sheep for the slaughter. Nay, in all these things we are more than conquerors through Him Who loved us" (Rom. 8:35-37). Despite this, with the prayers of the Fathers and our hope in the Ruler of our faith, our Lord Jesus Christ, and through the intercessions of the most blessed Theotokos and ever-virgin Mary, we went through fire and water fighting the good fight. We hope, holy Hierarchs, that through your own petitions and prayers, we will find mercy according to the Master's command, "Come to me, all you who labor and are heavy laden, and I will give you rest" (Matt. 11:28).

Your Eminences, Holy Hierarchs, and my venerable Fathers and brethren, we put your initial thought to rest with the patristic saying: "Remove temptation, and no one will be saved."

From what we know, the blessed Elder, with this very thought, endured all the temptations which the all-working divine Providence allowed in his life without complaint, like another Job, and we wish to believe that in the end, God rewarded him very richly. If, as a man, he unwillingly embittered any brother of our Sacred Skete, then from our own lowliness we request that we forgive him according to the Lord's Prayer, so that the Law of God may be fulfilled: "Bear one another's burdens, and so fulfill the Law of Christ" (Gal. 6:2).

But we will also forgive, my venerable Fathers and brethren, because perhaps at some point in our spiritual struggle, we involuntarily embittered him. One thing is certain, that "while alive" he prayed for all the Fathers from his heart, and rejoiced like a guileless child at the spiritual progress of the Fathers and rest of the brothers.

Pray, Your Eminences, Holy Metropolitan of Demetriados and Holy Metropolitan of Ierissos, that we who remain may also be granted to imitate the godly and God-bearing life and example of the Holy Elder Anthimos, whose brief biography we present.

He was born on November 5, 1913 in the village Kallianoi of Corinthia of pious parents, and he was named Constantine.

After he graduated from the Academy, he was tonsured as a monk on November 21, 1930 by Elder Gabriel Lambis from Madyton, the distinguished Hieromonk and

Spiritual Father of the Sacred Skete of St Anne on the Holy Mountain.

He was ordained as a deacon at the Kyriakon of the Sacred Skete of St Anne by Metropolitan Hierotheos of Militoupolis on April 13, 1933.

He was ordained priest at the Kyriakon of the Skete of St Anne by Metropolitan Hierotheos of Militoupolis on August 24, 1936.

In the Metropolitan chapel of the Sacred Metropolis of Thessalonica, Metropolitan Panteleimon (Papageorgiou) of Thessalonica elevated him to the rank of Archimandrite for his Sacred Kalyva, and made him Spiritual Father of the Sacred Skete of St Anne.

He reposed on June 28, 1996 at 6:00 in the afternoon at the 424 Military Hospital of Thessalonica due to heart failure. The burial and funeral service was chanted the next day at the Sacred Skete of St Anne.

He was the Spiritual Father of many monks and lay people, a wise, humble, meek, discerning, quiet-loving and service-loving Elder. He was an excellent liturgist, a work-loving iconographer, and a good and hospitable Dikaios."

Uncovering the Precious Relics

The sacred Chrysostom mentions that "whoever has the correct faith and a pure life is holy." Elder Anthimos fulfilled both these conditions of Chrysostom, so we should have no doubts about his holiness. People, of course, expect incorruption of the body, myrrh to flow from the bones, miracles and healings during the exhumation, as a confirmation of the holiness of the reposed. Those who are more moderate, and the Hagiorites for the most part, consider the yolk-colored yellow hue of the bones to be an indication of the soul's salvation. The whole matter of holiness, of course, belongs to the divine will and none of us earthly creatures knows the fathomless judgments of the Lord. The only thing we know is that the indwelling of the grace of the All-Holy Spirit for many years in the souls of the Saints is imparted also to their earthly flesh and to those bones, so that many times they satisfy people's expectations. The measure of holiness is not given only by signs, however. Furthermore, the time of the Saints' miracle working is not firm. The Lord gives this gift when He wishes to honor the virtue of the Saint, and to set him up as a model in a faltering society.

For three years the venerable body of the Elder Anthimos rested in the earth of the Skete of St Anne. Three years after his venerable repose, the quietness of his tomb was disturbed, and his holy bones were brought into the light of day. For 83 years they held upright a soul which worked diligently for the glory of the All-Holy name of our Christ, and for the salvation of many people.

On June 15/28, 1999 the Elder's tomb was opened and his golden yellow bones were collected with much reverence, and quite a few people noticed a fragrance. Since that time, they have been treasured in the church of the Entrance of the Theotokos of his Kalyva, for the sanctification of those who draw near and venerate them with faith. Metropolitan Nikodemos of Ierissos presided at the three year memorial service which followed. He knew the Elder and had clear proofs of his holiness. Furthermore, during Vespers which he served at the church of the Entrance, manifestly moved with joy, he commemorated the Elder Anthimos with the saints at the dismissal.

Among other things, the holy Metropolitan of Ierissos said in a trembling voice, "Of course the blessed soul of the Holy Elder, foretasting unending comfort in the bosom of Abraham and awaiting the final Judgment, blesses all those who fight the good fight, and who honor him." Meanwhile, the hieromonk Elder Makarios, Dikaios of the Skete who was present, the members of his Brotherhood, and the rest of the Fathers and the lay brethren inwardly murmured, "Saint! Saint!"

II.
Teachings of the Elder Anthimos

Monasticism, a Constant Restraining of Nature

Our ancient forebears had based their lives on firm foundations. The moment for the Incarnation of our Lord had not come, and their philosophy had other principles. Since the joyous message that "no one can lay any other foundation than that which is laid, which is Jesus Christ" (1 Cor. 3:11) had not been heard yet, they built the foundations of society on other, but firm foundations and taught "think as a mortal and be as forbearing as an immortal." The Christ-centered life, of course, and the heartfelt love of the Savior Christ lift man to other spheres. It gives him a foretaste of the good things which the Lord has prepared for those who love Him.

Monasticism which is associated with this undiminished and unending love of man for his Creator, has its beginning in apostolic times. The blessed Elder used to say teaching, 'As St Dionysios the Aeropagite (October 3), the boast of Athens, mentions, monks were called healers or physicians. Therefore, he addressed himself (Letter 8) to a certain lover of stillness and vigilance, whom he calls "Demophilos the Healer." They were servants of Jesus and remained outside of the cities and the villages and helped the bishops and the presbyters in spreading the Gospel. Dionysios the Aeropagite, the Apostle, philosopher, hierarch and martyr, adorned with all the virtues, mentions these things, as we have said. So when the Gospel had been spread, these physicians took refuge in the desert, as did St Chariton the Confessor (September 28). After he was released from prison, he left his home and went to Palestine and founded monasteries. Then we have the boast of monasticism, St Anthony the Great (January 17), who ascended to the very heights of virtue, and in his life surpassed even the virtue of the Angels. Much later on, the monasticism of Athos came into being. The Holy Mountain, which is called 'the Garden of the Panagia', is next to the garden of God. The monks from the one garden go over to the other one, to God's eternal garden. Every day I, a sinner, entreat the Panagia and all the Saints of the Holy Mountain who came face to face with the Panagia and receive her promises, that I may also make this passage. Just as she promised St Peter the Athonite that she would be the helper, guardian and protectress of the monks, I ask her now to extend her protection to guard all Orthodox Christians and especially our pious nation, which showed forth millions of martyrs, monastic Saints, hierarchs, and even to our day continues showing forth sanctified personalities which support it and guide it on the safe path of salvation.

All monks live the violence of nature. They live the definition which monasticism has: 'The body works in order to be fed, the soul is vigilant in order to inherit.' Some are at higher levels of virtue, and others at lower levels. However, according to the promise of the Panagia, people who will struggle and expect the Kingdom of Heaven will not cease to be found until the end of the age. Of course, if the All-Good God applied His justice, all of us would have vanished from the face of the earth; but as He said to the Patriarch Abraham, 'if ten righteous people are found in the five cities (Sodom, Gomorrah, Sechor, etc.), I will not destroy them' (Genesis 18:32). Of course, only Lot and his family were found. Here, however there are many on the Holy Mountain, in the desert of Sinai, in the area of Holy Zion, where our Lord lived, was crucified and resurrected and everywhere that Orthodox monasticism exists, there are clergyman, monks and hierarchs who endure all hardships and pray for all of humanity. Because of their prayers God's goodness does not destroy us. He spares us for the sake of this little prayer, which we compare to the faltering speech of infants. You see, parents rejoice with the faltering speech of the infant who cannot speak, and are pleased and glorify God Who gave them a living image of themselves.

"In our day, I assure you, that many saints will come out of the big cities, from within the apartment buildings, the noise, the pollution and the agony of earthly cares. There are charismatic people who do violence to their nature and live a virtuous life more than some ascetics who live in the desert. To them the saying applies: 'It is not the place which sanctifies, but the manner of life.' You see, forcefulness of the body breaks the bonds of sin and frees the intellect. It allows it to fly near the throne of God's unapproachable glory, and to rejoice with the joy of the Angels."

Remembrance of Death, Remembrance of God

The phrase of Abba Evagrios in the *Gerontikon*: "Always remember eternal judgment and do not forget your departure, and no fault shall be imputed to your soul" was deeply carved into the soul of Elder Anthimos. He used to say, 'By the daily repetition of this phrase, we restrain the weakening of our zeal and of falling into sin. Our mind must be turned to seek God and ceaselessly commemorate the final Judgment of our justly judging Lord. Only thus will our passions be tamed and wiped out. The memory of death is inextricably associated with the fear of God. We drive Him far away from us when we do not contemplate death and the punishment which awaits us. When we do not pay attention to ourselves, when we do not examine how we spent the day, what we did, in what we transgressed, but we live indifferently and keep company with spiritually indifferent people.'

"The three things which help a person preserve virtue in his soul are mourning, tears for sins, and the constant remembrance of death. He who considers the day he is living as the last one of his life will not sin. O woe to us, because while we flee from this world in which we dwell as something temporal and temporary, for many years we are bound with worries and cares for corrupt and worldly things. When the moment comes for our absolutely necessary trip without return from this world, then we will not be able to take with us even one thing of all for which we strove. O woe to us, because, although it is certain that we will give an account before the King Christ for all the actions of our earthly life, for vain talking, for despondency, for our wicked and impure thoughts, we are not interested in our soul. We are irresponsible and indifferent.

"For Elder Anthimos, the memory of death was identified with the memory of God, and the spiritual gladness which this recollection grants to the souls of believers. Of the believers who reached high measures of virtue and do not fear and do not worry about the fearsome moment of their departure which does not lead to death, since it is a certain transport "from death to life" (John 5:25). Furthermore, Fr Anthimos, who had spent himself in love for God and neighbor, could shout together with Paul: "I have fought the good fight.... Henceforth, the crown of righteousness is laid up for me" (2 Timothy 4:8), the hour of death was desired. He awaited it with joy, because he was leaving the world of vanity, to pass to the opposite shore, to the world of incorruption. 'I desire to depart and be with Christ' (Philippians 1:23) he would say, showing thus his desire to depart this life and to be together eternally with his beloved Deliver and Savior of the world.

Our Duty to Fast

Elder Anthimos believed and lived the concept that the aim of fasting is for man to be freed from the iniquitous tyranny of the flesh, from handing over the spirit to the flesh of clay and its urges, which is the tragic result of sin and of the original fall of man. "Only with careful and patient effort", he used to say, "does man discover that 'he shall not live by bread alone' (Luke 4:4) and he brings back within him the priority of the spirit. Fasting is nothing other than a true practical challenge for the head liar, the Devil, who manages each time to convince us that we are dependent only on bread and to build the whole of human knowledge, secular science and all our existence on this lie. Fasting is a real struggle against the devil. The continent and fasting person sweetens his mouth with the prayer of the heart. He feels many times as if he's holding fistfuls of sugar in it, or as if he's eating very sweet honey, as the great Prophet David also says, *"How sweet to my throat are Thy words, more than honey to my mouth"* (Ps. 118/119:103). Fasting, from the viewpoint of health, is beneficial." The Elder continues, "God knows what He has created, man, in other words, and for this reason He gave him fasting, which is helpful for health. Our ancient forebears, the Greek idolaters, had complete abstinence from food twice a week, on Monday and Thursday. The Holy Apostles changed these days and appointed Wednesday and Friday for fasting. We fast on Wednesday because the betrayal of Christ took place on this day. Did you see who betrayed? The disciple betrayed the

Teacher! Creation betrayed the Creator! The Evil One betrayed the infinite Benefactor, and on a Friday. Oh, how very dreadful, very fearsome! The earth was shaken. The sun was darkened. The rocks were split asunder. The tombs were opened. We, rational people and Christians, shouldn't we fast? Should we become worse than the rocks and other lifeless things, which witnessed on the day of the Passion, as St Dionysios the Areopagite (October 3) says, that a dreadful eclipse of the sun took place at noon time, a scientifically inexplicable event, and he cried out, 'Either everything is coming to an end, or God is undergoing suffering.'

We Greeks should not forget that we are a nation to which God gave the wisdom to go to God with wisdom. But our ancestors misused the high gift of wisdom and worshiped creation rather than the Creator, and investigated all creation. Yes, it is natural, because knowledge of God is a divine revelation which our ancestors did not have and for this reason, when they heard that in Jerusalem there was a man, a phenomenon Who with a simple word healed every illness, chased away every chastisement from humanity, opened the eyes of those who were born blind and raised the dead, they realized that this was not a human being, but God. Then a whole delegation left Greece and went to hear Him, as John says in his Gospel: 'Certain Greeks approached Philip, who was from Bethsaida of Galilee, and said to him, «Sir, we wish to see Jesus» (John 12:21). Philip then told the Apostle Andrew, whose offspring we are, and presented them to Jesus, Who immediately cried out, 'Now the hour has come for the Son of man to be glorified' (John 12:23).

So, our ancestors, those idolaters, labored so much and went to Jerusalem before the saving Passion of our

Redeemer. They remained there, they saw all the events, and after Pentecost, came and proclaimed them. We, their descendants, should we not imitate them and labor a bit with fasting, which strengthens the body and enlivens the soul? Is this difficult? We see that the ascetics, who fast in a fearful way, are all long-lived, whereas those who seek pleasure, who eat ceaselessly, live for few years and are afflicted with many illnesses. The medicine for the best health and the increase of virtue, which safeguards man from every attack of evil, is fasting. The Ninevites entreated God with fasting, and as the Prophet Jonah mentions, they escaped destruction. The same prophet was sitting beneath a gourd and waited to see the outbreak of God's wrath. Suddenly, then, the gourd dried up and the prophet was very deeply saddened. Then he heard God censure him saying, 'I see that you are saddened for the gourd which dried up, and which you did not toil to plant. It sprouted on its own, came up and made shade. Shall I not take pity upon on Nineveh, that great city, in which so many people dwell, who do not know their right hand or their left? Everyone remained fasting, from the King and the elderly down to the infants and the animals. How can I not take pity on them?' (Jonah 4:11).

Do you see how fasting not only grants a multitude of good things to man, but also propitiates God Himself. The idea which some people have, that fasting is harmful, is a delusion. Whoever does hard work must eat something in order to be strengthened, and also the sick people, should follow the advice of the doctors. In these cases our body needs special treatment, for it is 'a temple of the Holy Spirit within us' (I Corinthians 6:19).

Youth and an Ecclesiastical Outlook

An experienced Spiritual Father, Father Anthimos confessed a multitude of young people, who took refuge in his counsels, since he knew their problems well. He agonized for them. He agonized for the future of the youth with their modern views, apostasy and indifference. In his prayer he always kept the youth in his thoughts, and fervently entreated the Lord to guide them on the correct path, on the path of duty and keeping His commandments.

He often would say giving lessons in physiology, 'Until the age of sixteen, man's mind is imperfect, and for this reason falls into many transgressions. In this day and age, parents must bring their children up "in the discipline and admonition of the Lord" (Eph. 6:4). If children are taught the correct things by their parents and are placed on a firm footing and enter the straight and true road which safeguards the body's health and lifts the soul to the divine likeness, then they will have constant success in their life and will live in a healthy way, because some are neuropathic from the abuses of their foolishness, and others schizophrenic. To prevent all these sick conditions we must have "life in Christ" as our model and be close to the Church, which is our common Mother. She is the Kingdom of God, the Body of Christ. We must subject ourselves to Christ, the head of our Church, just as our body is subject to the head. If young people return and submit to Christ, they will be saved, as He Himself assured, "those who return to me, I shall heal" (Matt. 13:15).

"Today young people have an egotistical outlook. They do not easily agree to submit to the Church. Every youth has his own understanding. All of them are unsubmissive and blind. As the Lord says, "If a blind person leads a blind person, both shall fall into a pit" (Matt. 15:14). Fortunately many of them later recovered after they traversed the crooked and contrary path of life, the path of evil. Now, for this reason a multitude of young people come to the Holy Mountain, and they reap the fruits of Christianity, and are made firm in faith. They become, let's say, the formerly corrupt, let us say, become chaste and good and those who had formerly gone astray, come to the path of life and again become members of our Church, by the grace of Christ. They suffered, and having suffered and hated the passions, they recover and become chaste.

"They become more steadfast than those who have not suffered. The Almighty God, Who made the invisible Angels and all visible things on the earth, made heaven, and made man "in His image and likeness" (Genesis 1:26), like the father in the parable of the Prodigal Son, awaits the return of his unruly children. The first Adam, through his egotism, brought us here to the land of weeping, to the land of exile. We must become children of the second Adam, of our Lord Jesus Christ, go up to heaven, to our real homeland and see His glory and the awesome beauty of His All-Holy face. Of course, one cannot conceive of a return without the Church and without a sacramental life. The Church is the Body of Christ. Her head is the Lord Himself. The body can do nothing without the head. Did you understand me? No matter how much a young person toils, he will not be saved outside the Church! The Lord said, 'without me you can do nothing' (John 15:5). Whoever recovers from the intoxication of sin and changes the evil path he is walking and asks God to help him, He will not refuse His help. He has promised us that, if we ask Him, He will hasten to come to our aid, "for everyone who asks receives, and he who seeks finds, and to him who knocks it shall be opened" (Matt. 7:8). "Whoever asks for something very fervently, I will give it to him, and I will open the door of my compassion to whoever knocks on it and demands my undivided help and protection." These words of God leave no doubt about His quick help, as long as we ask Him for it.

From Being in the Image to Being in the Likeness

"Man is God's preeminent creation. He surpasses all the other creatures, because the Invisible, the Incomprehensible, the Indescribable Lord in His omnipotence, His omniscience, His strength, has created man thus in a two-fold way, 'in the image and in the likeness of God' and according to the sense, as is the other creation, the material one. He is in the image because God is Spirit and man is spirit, God is everywhere present, and man goes everywhere with his intellect. God created everything that we see and everything that we don't see. The things we see are corrupt; those we don't see are incorrupt, eternal. Man sees his body, because it is matter, which is comprised of five elements (earth, water, air, fire and air). Bones come from the earth, and liquids, such as the blood, come from the water. The temperature of the body comes from fire. From the air come all the airy components which circulate in the blood, such as the oxygen which is necessary for oxygenation. From the ether come the components of breath and of smell, which breathes and provides life. Of course, all the animals and man have these. Man, however, has an element which he can neither perceive, nor reject. He has a spirit, which we call soul. This spirit is an essence, it does not have five parts as the body does, and it is this which gives excellence to man. The animals have senses. Man also has senses which the animals have, but he also has an intellect. The most royal sense of man is sight, which sees everything around him. The other animals also have this sense. The most obvious energy of the soul, which the animals don't have, however, is the intellect, the eye of the soul. For this reason, he goes everywhere with the intellect. As with the eyes he sees all existing things around him, so with the intellect he sees all the noetic things. God creates, man also creates. He creates from matter. Without matter he can't do anything. He creates and builds houses, cars, tools, ships, airplanes. He makes cars and runs faster than the rabbits and the foxes. He makes ships in the sea, makes submarines to go in the sea together with the fish. He makes diving suits to go down to the bottom with the shellfish. He flies high in the sky, above the clouds where the birds do not go. He has reached up to the moon. Can any other living organism except man do all these things? You see, they bear witness to man being created 'in the image.'

"'In the image' is, let us say, simpler, sensory. From man's conception he has intellect, reason and spirit. Intellect is the Father, reason is the Son and spirit is the divine Comforter. They are not tangible beings, but we can't deny them, since they become sensory. So he has lost being 'in the image' because of the transgression of the first-created people. For this reason being 'in the image' is of no benefit if we don't ascend to being 'in the likeness', because like unites with like. Light is united with light, can light unite with darkness? No, so it is! My own hand and the hand of a brother are united, because they are similar. Can we grasp the hand of the icon, or can the icon grasp our own hand? No! For this reason, if we don't ascend to being 'in the likeness', it would have been better that we were not born. Because if man lives even a thousand years, which no one has done, then he has no end. Because the soul and the spirit are indivisible, are eternal, are immortal, are logical.

That indivisible, the immortal, the logical feels fear and wants to take refuge in the protection of an almighty spirit. Just as the children run to parents, thus each one of us runs to the Father of spirits, our Creator and God. Yes! But we are creatures! Just as each thing which man builds cannot understand man, neither can we understand the incomprehensible Creator. We can understand only a portion of His divine energies, as many as were revealed to the Patriarchs, to the Prophets, to His incarnate economy. Just as our own work can't understand us, let's say, so we cannot understand God. Not like some deceived people, not to say crazy people, who left the earth's orbit and wanted to see God! I don't know what they took Him for. Did they imagine Him as a cloud, or some light? God is infinite, incomprehensible in essence, indescribable, unthinkable, above every position. Just as we make an object and are outside of it, so God is outside the world we see, because He is the creator of the world. Just as a building cannot understand anything about us, so also creation cannot understand God, except whatever God Himself revealed to us. Just as our own work bears witness to our energy, the toil we did, our wisdom with which we made it, so man also bears witness to his almighty God, the incomprehensible and indescribable. Man has the power to see, but what must He be Who gave His creatures the power of sight? He sees even the most utmost depths of our soul and, whatever happens everywhere. This almighty Godhead created hearing. Yet, what must the hearing of the almighty God be? He hears even the most intimate parts of man's soul and, if they are pleasing to God, they are rewarded, if not, they are condemned. This almighty God created everything in the sphere of the senses and of those things seen. How super-perfect he is! So the weak man must understand that he is a weak creature and should approach his Creator, to secure himself, and not fall into deceptive destruction. He should guard the health of his body and the immortality which his soul has, that is the capability of inheriting eternity. Because, let's say, he doesn't have another year from the present life, to ascend to being 'in the image.'

Let's see now how from being 'in the image' we can go to being 'in the likeness', how can we can unite with God, because like is united with like, as we said. So first He tells us, 'Become ye holy, for I am Holy' (1 Peter 1:16). We must all struggle to become holy, as much as possible. What, however, is holiness? Holiness, for us, is to cast off evil and to do what is good. He says, 'The Lord is righteous and loved righteousness' (Psalm 10/11:8). So, let righteousness begin from our own person. Let us give to our soul the things which belong to her, let us give her primarily principles. In this way we will lead her to eternity and to immortality. Let us not forget that the soul acts as a tool and is responsible for whatever the body does. For this reason we must also give the body its normal nourishment and its normal clothing and not let it completely destroy the soul in an irrational manner. The soul dominates the body. First we think and decide and then the body acts. For this reason we will also give account for every word, every action, our every thought. So, once we give just things to our own self, to our soul, in other words faith, perfection, good works etc., we will also give the same to the body, which demands food and clothing. Whatever we do to those around us, we must love it and it should be identified with whatever we want others to do to us. This is a command of our incarnate Lord, of the God-man Jesus Christ. "Whatsoever you wish people to do to you must also do to them" (Matt. 7:12). Do we want other people to love us? Let us also love them. Do we want them to beat us, to hurt us? No! No one wants it! Then neither should we do harm to anyone. This is the perfect expression of love, the fulfillment of divine law, which is not found anywhere else, except in the sacred Gospel.

"So, again he says: 'Become compassionate, as your Father is compassionate' (Luke 6:36). He makes his 'sun to rise on the evil and on the good, and sends rain on the just and on the unjust.' (Matt. 5:46). Let us also imitate the kindness of the compassionate God, and love the good; let us also forgive those who harm us, who badly take advantage of us and look down on us, and pray for their salvation. If we love only those who love us, we are not doing anything more than the publicans and sinners do, and we will not have grace from God. The commandment of our Lord, which covers all the other commandments, is clear: 'Love your enemies' (Luke 6:35). Then we absolutely observe the will of God and become real images of God. He created us body and soul. From the soul He wants true faith, from reason, truth, and from the body, chastity and purity. Because He says: the body is the temple of the Holy Spirit, and if anyone defiles the temple of God, "God shall destroy him" (1Corinthians 3:17). So in order for us to see the face of God, we must pursue our sanctification, keeping our bodies free from every impropriety.'

Exhortations to Married and Unmarried People

"Let married people be chaste and perform the work which they themselves selected, i.e. child-bearing. With this work they become colleagues of God through the recreation of humanity. They are, let's say, molds which God uses, for the human kind to be made eternal. If they do not remain firm in the work which they selected to perform, they sin and fall and will be under trial of judgment and inherit eternal hell.

"Unmarried people, those who are real celibates, want to ascend high, above every sense, coercing their soul and pursuing that which is 'above nature.' Married people have marriage, which the beasts also have, whereas celibates want celibacy, which the Angels also follow. They try to live the life of the bodiless Angels, even though they are in the flesh, which is something arduous and wearisome. For this very reason, however, they also have great rewards from

God. The Angels are immaterial natures, rational and ministering spirits sent out as servants of people, who will inherit the Kingdom of Heaven with the purpose of rousing their thoughts for salvation. The monks who promised celibacy are imitators of Angels, they are equal to the Angels and teach people by their word and work , that is, what they must do to enjoy the eternal good things. Monks, like the Angels, ceaselessly hymn God night and day. Angels have love and monks put love into practice, not only within their narrow milieu, but also to the whole human race, because "Christ is the light of Angels, Angels are a light for monks, and monks are a light for all people' (*Ladder* 26:31). He ought to complete well each proportional path he has chosen, so that he might receive just praise and recompense from the prize-bestowing Lord, Who distributes prizes to His faithful servants. Unfortunately, however today everything has been perverted and, as the divine Chrysostom says: 'the high have become the low, people instead of looking upward, and behaving as they should, looking upward, which means I look at the things above, they look down at their passions, debauchery, impiety, hypocrisy, prodigality, and dissipation.' A few remain, however, as the almighty God says in His dialogue with the Patriarch Abraham, and for this reason humanity is still preserved. God preserves it for the sake of those few, despite the wretched state which has arrived today, since they lead a life worse than the animals, the wild beasts and beasts. For this reason, I also cried out with the Prophet Jeremiah:

""Who shall give water to my head and a fountain of tears to my eyes? Then I would weep for this my people day and night' (Jer. 8:23); How can I lament the wretched state of the people of my race, of the formerly wise Hellenes, or of the Orthodox Christians, my brethren in the flesh and in spirit? All true Christians are called Orthodox, because we have the teaching of Jesus and are struggling to live according to it. We are children of the font, because there we are adopted, there we are reborn. We become one body, since we eat the body of Christ and become one body with Him. We become the same blood, since we drink Christ's blood and become one blood with Him. We obtain the same mind, since we become one mind with Christ. We are for all these one body and ought to love one another, as the Lord appoints "love your neighbor as yourself" (Matt. 22:39). Of course, this love is not related to that which is practiced by the heretics, the atheists and the deceivers of the people. Real love is based on the foundation of truth and righteousness. This last one says that everything, a tract of land or an object, belongs to someone. It is love for someone to give us something in order to do us a favor, and then for us to return it to him, since we do not take anything with us and others may be helped by the use of this thing. This is real love and not false love which neglects the truth, and is based on falsehood, injustice and sin. In other words, it is based on the qualities which the Lord, the very personification of love, abhors and hates. As the Evangelist John says, 'God is love' (1 John 4:8). Let our struggle for the building of our salvation be based on the foundation of faith, my brethren. Let this become the firm ground, the suitable land for the building of our salvation. Without land we cannot build a house and without true faith we cannot be saved, the house of our soul cannot be saved.

Concerning Repentance

"Repentance is the renewal of Baptism. For this reason, a person makes promises at Baptism, or a godparent promises for him, so also at repentance, once he admits his faults, he also promises not to commit them again. God's infinite compassion gave us this Mystery of Repentance and canceling our wicked faults, so that we can be saved and can partake of unending blessedness. Our repentance cleanses us and makes us sinless again. It whitens the defiled robe of our soul and puts the robe of incorruption on us. It is a new covenant with God, and for this reason he says: 'He who is baptized and believes shall be saved, while he who disbelieves shall be condemned' (Matt. 16:16). Then, he who transgresses in something and repents is cleansed from his filth, his faults are forgiven and he is saved. There is no greater example than St Mary of Egypt (April 1). She transgressed greatly, her flesh became a vessel of pleasure, she led a multitude of pleasure-loving men to perdition, but with repentance she ascended the whole ladder of virtues. She surpassed in virtue even those Angels. While in the body, St Mary walked on the surface of the river Jordan like an incorporeal being. She reached measures of holiness, the Angels were afraid, the demons trembled, and people marveled and still marvel. For this reason we have her as an example of practical repentance. No matter how much we transgress, we repent and are justified with God's grace. We offer repentance, God the grace. He renews us, He cleanses us, He saves us, according to His infinite mercy. This was also the purpose of His incarnation. He told it to us: 'I did not come to call the righteous, but sinners to repentance' (Matt. 8:13).

Repentance is very easy. It lies within man's intention. St Mary of Egypt could not enter the church in Jerusalem, because some invisible power pushed her away. As soon as she recognized her offenses, she repented. She fell on her knees; she cried and chose the Lady Theotokos as the intercessor and guarantor of her repentance. Then she got up and entered into the church, venerated the Precious Cross, and then embarked on a life of repentance and ceaseless asceticism. We people must realize and become aware that we are only dust and ashes. A moment comes when the soul is separated from the material body, and this fear of perceived death startles people and leads them to repentance. Confession follows after this. The All-Good God did not appoint Angels to accept the errors of men. He appointed people who suffer the same things, bishops and priests, who are successors of the Apostles. The Apostles of Christ received all authority as He told them, 'As the Father sent me, I also send you' (John 20:21). Once He breathed on them, He continued, 'Receive the Holy Spirit. Whosoever sins you remit, they are remitted to them. Whosoever sins you retain, are retained' (John 20:21-23).The Holy Apostles passed on this authority of remitting sins to their successors, and they subsequently passed it down to Orthodox priests who are Father Confessors, and they will pass it down to the close of the ages.

"Man's disposition, as we mentioned, is the power of the soul which dominates the body, and of the body which follows the soul. For this reason, if they transgress, both the soul and the body will be condemned in eternal hell. In the Symbol of our faith (Creed) we say that we look for the resurrection of the dead, where the sinners will proceed to the eternal fire, which 'is prepared for the devil and his angels' (Matt. 25:42), and the righteous will inherit the 'kingdom prepared from the foundation of the world' (Matt. 25:34). So we have no excuse, we will go wherever we want, either to unending joy and life, or to eternal affliction and damnation. The disposition goes hand in hand with the judgment which man possesses. All people are rational beings. Logic gives birth to judgment, and judgment gives birth to the advantage of each person. Everyone has a disposition. Even infants have a disposition. For this reason, when they see their parents, they run to them with joy, but when they see people they do not know, they run away and cry."

The Slip of Young People
Into False Religions

"Our Orthodox faith is a spring with abundant crystal clear water 'welling up to eternal life' (John 4:14). Unfortunately, however, few of our young people depart from the clear spring and go to the dirty pits to find water to drink. Here the saying of the Apostle Paul applies: 'Bad company corrupts good morals' (1 Cor. 15:33). Our young people who keep company with various people of other religions are swayed, because they are not catechized in the faith, like dead fish which go wherever the current of the river takes them. For this reason the Evangelist John forbids us to keep company with those who don't have the teaching of Jesus and don't live in accordance with it. We should not even greet them, nor receive them in our homes, so that we don't become partakers of their impiety. He orders us: 'Whoever comes to us and does not bear the teaching of Christ, do not receive him into your home, and do not greet him' (2 John 10-11).

We Orthodox do not believe simply or by chance. Nor do we sacrifice our life and all the joys of the world for a faith and a truth whose correctness we have not examined. Each one of us has his home, his estate, his plot of land. We confirm all these things through the contracts we have and the witnesses we have. For confirmation in faith we have the Old Testament, which was translated into Greek three hundred years before the birth of Christ, and furthermore by Jews, who are opponents of Christ. While as witnesses we have those who saw with their own eyes the miracles of the God-man Jesus. First the Apostles and then the Greeks who went to meet Him, and they saw the victory of His Resurrection, of His Ascension into the heavens and the indwelling of the All-holy Spirit on His disciples. Christ's Resurrection shows us the almightiness of the Godhead, because no mortal can resurrect on his own. By His Resurrection Our Lord trampled upon the dominion of the devil, defeated Hades and gave joy to His disciples, with whom He remained for forty days. In His Ascension to the heavens, which took place before everyone, Angels with a white garment told the disciples, 'O men of Galilee, why do you stand looking at the sky? This Jesus who was taken up from you into heaven shall come in the way you saw him proceeding to heaven' (Acts 1:11). Jesus will come again, O Galileans, in the same wondrous manner you saw Him ascend to heaven. God gave power to those simple and unlettered fishermen, so that although unarmed, they subjugated the whole universe. Neither Caesars, nor philosophers, nor false conceited people were able to oppose the power of the words of the Gospel of love which the Apostles had as their weapons. For this reason for two thousand years now Christ reigns, and Him crucified.

"Two things push young people to abandon Orthodoxy and to go to Eastern religions. The first is ignorance, and second wicked curiosity. Don't you see that even those fakirs come here to the Holy Mountain to see the real divinization (theosis) of man? They should understand that the absolute destiny of man is to ascend to being 'in the likeness' and to unite with God. If he does not achieve it, it is better that he were not born, because he will not be benefited even if he lives for a thousand years, (which no one has done), for he has unending hell as his end. Young people go to deceptions in order to calm themselves from the censure of conscience. They go there to find another God, who tolerates impurity, filth, absurdity and falsehood, as Mohammed also says, to find themselves in a prosperous paradise, where for centuries they will eat orzo, they will drink rivers of syrups and fornicate and commit lewd acts. Can dead people eat? Can they drink? Can they fornicate? Certainly not! So the young people easily believe these lies and are swayed, whereas you see even those logical fakirs of Tibet and of other parts of Asia come here to see the real theosis of man, how in other words he reaches being 'in the likeness.' He achieves it with forcefulness and asceticism according to the words of our Lord, 'The Kingdom of the Heavens suffers violence, and the violent take it by force' (Matt. 11:12). This, my beloved, is the path to the Kingdom of God. For us to force ourselves not to commit evil, and not to force ourselves to betray the Faith, to betray what is good, in order to be saved, apparently, eternally. We have the truth! Our young people must avoid the Sirens which temporally attract, but guide them to destruction. Christ is the only one who leads those who keep His commandments to the harbor of salvation, and our young people should take this message to heart."

Humanity in the
Last Rung of Sin

Today humanity is in its worst condition since the creation of the world. The path it is following is a path of decline, a path of corruption, a path of darkness, a path which leads to destruction. People with their abuses, and especially those who are carnal, suffer both rationally and physically. Their therapy is very difficult. Only the almighty and All-good God, through the intercessions of many Saints, who are an innumerable multitude here in Greece, and all the millions of Martyrs, Monastic Saints, Apostles and Confessors, may take pity on His people and give them enlightenment. Only in this way can man be corrected and walk correctly. God's mercy and compassion changes the world's dispositions. Today the condition of decay is worse than that of the age of

Sodom. The filth of sin has overflowed and flooded the world. I am sad for the perdition of such a multitude of souls. The philanthropic Lord came to the earth for this reason, to raise up His sinful creature to heaven. He gave us grace and took our sinful flesh and cleansed it and sanctified it and deified it. He put man to sit at the right of the throne of His majesty. How can we excuse ourselves for the ingratitude we show for His great compassion?

Today we have arrived at the very gate of the Second Coming of the Lord. When will it happen? Only God knows, no one else.

"The first sign of it which St Hippolytus of Rome (January30) gives us in his Commentaries is the country of the Jews. Listen to what he says:

'As our Lord Jesus Christ, the Son of God and God, united all the nations in one faith, so also the Antichrist shall gather the scattered race of the Jews.'

"This began to be realized in 1948.

"The second sign is related to the Temple of Solomon. As our Lord Jesus Christ, the Son and Word of the living God, "raised up the temple of His body" and arose from the dead, so the Antichrist will also raise up the razed temple of Solomon, in which according to the Apostle Paul (2 Thess. 2:4) he will proclaim himself God, he will lift himself above every worshipped thing and will sit in the temple of God with the claim that he is God. So, rebuilding the Temple of Solomon will come first and then the coming of the Antichrist will take place, whom 'the Lord shall slay with the spirit of His mouth and will abolish the appearance of His presence' (2 Thess. 2:8), in other words, He will destroy the Antichrist with the breath of His mouth and will abolish him by His appearance and His coming.

However, let's allow God to decide the time of His triumphant coming to earth, to judge the living and the dead. As for us, let us try to avoid sin, because this is real death, since it takes us far, it separates us from God, from true Life, from Light, from unending joy, from all good things. May the good God enlighten His creatures, and also the Greeks who "seek wisdom," (1 Cor. 1:23) but now go to the fakirs and the mediums who teach them foolishness instead of wisdom."

In This Place Every Step also has its Saint

"St Anne's Skete is Saint-nurturing. It has been enriched with the streams of tears and sweat of many ascetics who throughout the centuries have longed for perfection and theosis "in Christ." Each corner is sanctified by ancient and contemporary saints. It is worthwhile for us to remember a few as an example, and to imitate their very pure conduct.

"The reposed Joachim did not work miracles after death, but he did while he was alive. He was a robber chief from Crete, a thief against the Turks, but not against Christians. He murdered a Turkish administrator then hung him on a tree and the birds devoured him. The Turks severely held this against him and did the impossible possible in order to capture him. His name was John. Then good Christians came and took him out to Macedonia, where he remained in the fields of a Turk. There was a chapel there where he would go and pray. His master once saw him praying and chanting with the Angelic powers. He made a decision and brought him here to the Skete. Farther over is his cave where he lived in asceticism. Distinguished by simplicity, he wanted them to name him Anna. The Fathers, however, explained things to him, and he took the name of her husband Joachim. He remained in the cave for many years, and reposed around 1902. Before his death, being very elderly, he was transferred to the place of the new ossuary, where he reposed. He had great forcefulness in his life. After praying, he gave dry plums to Russian pilgrims. One father received them and gave them to his child, who was mute from his birth, to eat. When he placed them in his mouth, he spoke. To another he gave dried figs and he went and put them on the eyes of his blind child and he saw. The Russian church has printed icons of his, where he is depicted practicing asceticism in his cave.

In this place at every step there is a saint, an ascetic who reached up to dispassion and theosis. There were real workers of mystical theology, of continual prayer, like Damascene from Aivali of Asia Minor, who practiced asceticism here, a strict hesychast, who had great relations with our house. The blessed Damascene would take only thirty okas of wheat a year, when others wanted one hundred, and one hundred thirty. He once was tearing down a stone wall to fix it, and upon digging found the incorrupt relics of a reposed holy Father. It was night and he left the relics there until the morning, so he could go down to the Kyriakon to notify the priests to go with lanterns to take it, as befits the saints. Then the reposed Saint appeared to him and told him, 'Cover me up there where I am. We don't want glory even now. If you don't cover me up right away, I will punish you now, and even at the Judgment.'

"He covered him up there where he was, and he remains unknown. There are many phenomena here. Damascene also had great virtue. *"Hagiorite Hesychastic Monasticism"*, ascribed to a certain Cyril, is actually by Damascene, who reposed around 1915. The Elders have told me these things, since I came in 1929.

"There was a whole choir of such strict hesychasts, with prayer, work and strictness alone, isolated, practicing hesychasm. Damascene was all vigil, as Arsenios the Great says, one hour of sleep in 24 hours. Elder Damascene was a great hesychast. Various people see mystical lights lighting up in various places. Of the 600 monks we have here, every cave also has a hesychast. Nevertheless, if he did not completely attain theosis, he reached dispassion, which is a lower level of foresight, as St Gregory the Theologian defines. All these are holy men. Here in our Kalyva lived a virtuous Elder Dositheos, who was granted to see Angels. This was before the Elder Theophilos, who lived to be one hundred twenty years old, took it. He came in 1828 and reposed in 1918. He was forceful, and for twenty years he slept only two hours a day.

"There were such people, like the holy Dositheos here. St Savvas of Kalymnos is a disciple of our Kalyva. I did not meet him, Theophilos met him. For this reason when we learned about him, we went to his monastery in Kalymnos in 1960. He was tonsured a monk by his Elder James, and studied painting here. After his death, where the Elder John remained as his successor, St Savvas went to Jerusalem. He came here again as a priest. Then he went again to Jerusalem, where he remained at the church of the

Resurrection, but more so he practiced asceticism in the monastery of Chozeba, as is mentioned in his biography. He was a very ascetical man. Then he went to Aigina with St Nektarios, from where he often came here. He visited the place for the last time in 1927, where he was given a treat here in the guest room.

"The holy monastic martyr Nektarios of Vryoulon in Asia Minor (July 11) was tonsured a monk in the Kalyva of St John the Theologian. His biography is clear. Holy Trinity, which is beneath the cemetery, is also an ancient Church, and there is the cave of St Gerasimos of Kephallonia. The saint's cousin, Germanos, appears in the codex of the Skete. He built the first Kyriakon of St Anne. His name in the world was George, and he was older than the Saint. The Saint was leaving from their Kalyva of the Annunciation and went to the cave for more struggles. Germanos was also virtuous. According to the custom, every five years, the Fathers would go to Jerusalem. The two cousins went together, and the Patriarch of Jerusalem kept St Gerasimos there.

"The chapels of the Kalyves were built in the sixteenth century. The recently reposed Elder Chrysanthos of Holy Trinity, dear Fathers, had as a Spiritual Father the niptic (watchful) Elder Onouphrios, Menas the Montenegran, and a certain Vincent. Elder Onouphrios came to the Holy Mountain on foot from Asia Minor. He reposed around 1918. He also went to the ruler of Montenegro and received help, then came and renewed the ancient Kalyva of the Transfiguration.

"I met Avimelech many years ago. He was quiet, prudent, monk and wrote about St Nektarios. Fr Savvas was a famous Spiritual Father of the utmost virtue. We shall see the true workers of the Lord at the Second Coming of God, those glorified by Him, as St Athanasios the Patriarch of

Constantinople said when monks asked him to declare a certain founder as a saint. He told them that we do not have any signs after his repose, as we have in other holy founders.

"I met the long-bearded Joachim. He came after me. He was of tall stature and his beard, which reached to the ground, he tucked into his cassock. Joachim reposed at a young age, he suffered from tuberculosis. A good brother, very pious, but not of a high spiritual stature, due to the lack of an experienced spiritual Elder, who is necessary for the cultivation of soul, wherein, through the grace of the Holy Spirit, the struggler ascends high.

"The story of our Kalyva is 150 years old. The story of our Skete is 1500 years old. Many saints passed through it."

*This text is an excerpt of a conversation with Elder Anthimos on June 28, 1982. It was published in the magazine "Protaton" vol. 15 page 34, January-February 1989.

III.
Wondrous Signs

Illumined by God and Humble

A young child from Thessalonica suffered from a deficiency of the kidneys. He constantly went for dialysis and his life was spent in pain and misfortune. His parents, pious people, were crushed. They couldn't bear to see their child suffering. The father voluntarily gave his own kidney so that his son would live. Unfortunately however, the patient's organism rejected the transplant and he weakened more. Again he went back on the waiting list, but they couldn't find a donor anywhere. The mother in her despair addressed herself to Fr Anthimos and in tears she explained their situation and received an answer. He himself spoke, but the words had a heavenly origin. The divine grace opened the lips of the humble Anthimos, who avoided men's praise, to say, "A donor will be found soon. He will be found in France."

The mother was confused by the Elder's answer and dared to ask, "How do you know this, Fr Anthimos?"

Immediately she received the answer from the ascetic who avoided men's glory, as the snares of the hater of good, "Balaam's ass spoke" (Num. 22:28).

"Soon a donor was actually found in France and the child, after the danger passed, now lives a normal life.

You Are Vasiliki's Daughter

The ten-year-old daughter of Mrs Vasiliki Kakouri was seeing the Elder for the first time at the hesychasterion of the Archangels in Vyrona. It seemed to her that he was shining, that he was engulfed by a bright light. She was not mistaken. Her very clear eyes, eyes which had not been defiled by sin, could see the uncreated light, the light which suffuses the Saints of our Church. She greeted him hesitant as she was, and he without having ever seen her before told her, "Come, my daughter. Aren't you Vasiliki's daughter?"

He Could See behind Buildings

The electrician Themistokles Katsoulis was going in the entrance of the hesychasterion of the Archangels in Vyrona. The Elder was sitting on the bench which is in the back part of the church, and was conversing with some visitor. The position of the church made it impossible to see the gate of the entrance. Fr Anthimos, however, was able to see even farther. His gaze passed through walls, just as X-rays go through a person's body. At a certain moment the Elder addressed the person with whom he was speaking and told him, "Go bring the man who is entering the door now here to me. I need him."

Let the Other Woman Come

Two friends, one of whom was being troubled by a demon, came to the hesychasterion of Vyrona where Fr Anthimos was giving spiritual talks. As soon as they went through the entrance, the possessed woman moved backwards. She was held back by the holiness of the place, just as St Mary of Egypthad once been, before she began her ascetic way of life which was equal to that of the angels. The other woman approached the Elder, who was inside the church and could not see the area outside. She bowed before him, but before she could speak the Elder said to her, "Call to me the other woman who came with you. I want to see her. She is worthy of our attention because she has been tormented by the primordially evil serpent who goaded our first parents, Adam and Eve."

You Will Have a Child

Mr Michael Vekris confessed to the Elder together with a friend of mine, he told him the problem he was facing. He wanted to have another child, but God did not consent to his wish. Seeing the purity of his motives and of his faith, the Elder told him, "You try again and I will pray for you to have a child. He who loosened the bonds of Elizabeth's barrenness and granted to her the precious Forerunner, and to us also; He who transformed the barren womb of St Anne, the protectress of our Skete, in order to grant us the most Holy Theotokos, who is more honorable than the Cherubim and more glorious than the Seraphim, He will also hear our petitions.

By God's grace and the prayers of Elder Anthimos, the humble couple actually had their much long-for child one year later.

The Snake Obeyed

In 1987, Mr Panagiotis Adamopoulos was living in poor circumstances when he and Elder Anthimos were coming up the uphill path which leads from the dock to the Kyriakon of St Anne. At a certain place, where the forest is dense and the path is hard to climb, an enormous snake appeared. "As soon as it saw us, it reared up high," he related, "and was getting ready to attack us. I froze. The Elder, however, calmly reassured me. Addressing the snake, he told it, 'Go over there on the other side'.

The snake lowered its head and, obeying the Elder, proceeded to its place and disappeared into the dense forest. The Saints, you see, are in harmony with irrational creation, the wild animals and reptiles. As spiritually renewed people of God, they have returned to the ancient beauty. Along with them creation also became tame, and it also sighs and suffers together with man who fell from Paradise. Irrational nature returns to a paradisiacal condition, placing itself at the service of man and obeying his orders. There are not a few such events, both ancient and more recent, where holy people had wild animals in their service, who obeyed all their orders like innocent and guileless lambs."

Utter Humility

Some indecent and evil-souled people dirtied the entrance to his Kalyva with filth in order to offend the Elder and test his forbearance and humility. As soon as he understood what happened he sadly shook his head at the fall of his brothers, and continued praying. Just as Christ girded Himself with a towel and washed the feet of His disciples (John 13:4), so the humble Anthimos also took the cleaning materials, and without murmuring cleansed the area of the filth and the stench. By his manner, he became an example to his subordinates, and also a reproach of their unwillingness to help with such "difficult" jobs.

He Calmed the Sea

Mr Panagiotis Gioules relates:

"The Elder was confessing at the Gregoriou Monastery. The little boat for St Anne's took me there with him. Before we arrived at its dock, however, a dreadful storm arose. He had not seen such a storm for sixty years, in other words as long as he was practicing asceticism on Athos. The little boat was riding deep in the water and began taking on water. The captains were scared. Then the Elder lifted his hands high and prayed fervently to Him who stops the swelling seas and tempests with a single gesture. His prayer lasted only a few seconds, but it was very fervent. Like a pillar of fire it ascended to the Throne of the Most High. Then he made the Sign of the Cross over the sea. It became calm only at that spot and down to the dock, while the storm was raging all around. He told the boat owners, 'Step on the gas, so that we can approach'.

So we docked, while the waves grew large and were breaking furiously against the shore and the terrible reefs."

A Theologian by Revelation

The Elder's wisdom and holiness of life gathered quite a few theologians next to him who sought documented answers to burning theological matters. The patrologists remain stunned before the depth of Fr Anthimos's knowledge. He may not have studied theology in universities; he was, however, a theologian "by revelation."

He Is a Child of the Panagia

Mr Theodore Poulopoulos had gone to the Holy Mountain with the doctor Mr Nikolaou, and the iconographer Mr Koustof. The Elder lovingly offered them hospitality like that of Abraham (Gen. 18:1-8), and in the morning after the service he began the discussion beneath the large extension. He related many spiritual things and developed theological topics. Among other things, he also spoke of a personal miracle. The person who heard it himself describes it as follows:

"There was a certain sick monk in New Skete. Fr Anthimos, who was always willing to contribute 'to the needs of the saints' (Rom. 12:13), took his little staff and went to visit him and to confess him. On the way back, there was a dreadful squall, and he was drenched. You see, on this road there is no place for one to be sheltered. His sweat from going uphill was mixed with the rain in the aged Elder's body, and he caught a cold. He went to his Kalyva and took to his ascetical bed, gravely ill with pneumonia. There where he was lying down, he saw the wall of his cell fall. He saw the sun brightly radiating. He saw two Angels coming to take his soul and one told the other one, 'Let's leave him a bit more. He has work to do!'. He also looked toward the region of Sithonia, however, and saw a multitude of demons drawing back like dogs. A very dark one, the leader, said, 'Get up and capture him who fights against us!'.

The other one got up and said, 'We can't capture him. He is a child of the Panagia!'

Then they disappeared."

Let's Tear Up our Degrees

After an extensive conversation with the Elder, a professor of the Theological School of the University of Thessalonica was saying:

"It's a good thing we don't have our degrees with us. If we did, we would have to tear them up. The Elder's knowledge has depth and breadth, theological depth and extensive breadth, covering every science. Naturally, these dimensions are not products of human wisdom, but of divine wisdom, since it is known that the Elder did not have the good fortune to obtain much education outside the monastery".

He Didn't Say Everything

The jaw surgeon Mr N. M. came to the Holy Mountainin the company of a priest. He asked to go to Confession to Fr Anthimos. He did not mention the burning subject which concerned him, the subject of blasphemy, at all. When the Confession was finished, the Elder turned to the priest who accompanied the penitent and told him, "You yourself did not tell me something very serious. His heart was not completely cleansed, but that's all right. Next year he will come again and will tell it to me."

The following year the same fellow did come back and confessed his transgression. From then on, by God's grace and the Elder's prayers, he cut it out as if with a knife.

They Won't Come Now, but Next Year

Two doctors, acquaintances of the Elder, Mr N.M and N. P. decided to go to the Holy Mountain with a priest they knew in order to visit him before the Christmas holidays. Furthermore, they set a date for the issuance of the Residence Permit. The priest considered it expedient to inform the Elder by telephone, so he could wait for them. Father Anthimos, however, saw something with his gift of foreknowledge and told him, 'The doctors won't come now, but in the summer.'

He was so persistent in his opinion that the priest backed down.

On the eve of the trip unexpected things did happen and the trip was delayed, just as the Elder had clearly foretold.

No One Is Harmed.
The Elder's Money

The doctor, Mr N.M., had operated on one of his patients at a private clinic. By mistake, the patient gave the doctor fifty thousand extra. When he realized the mistake, the doctor said, "This money is for Fr Anthimos."

After he sent it to him, he ascertained that there was another fifty thousand in his suit. In the meantime, the patient realized his mistake and asked the doctor to return the extra money, and he got it. Thus the Lord, Who provides everything "and honors the action and praises the disposition" (*Catechetical Homily of John Chrysostom*), gave to Fr Anthimos the portion which the doctor promised him, and no one was harmed.

He Heals Cancer

The father of a spiritual child of Fr Anthimos had cancer in the larynx. His doctors told him that it was inoperable. His condition was very advanced. With unspeakable grief his young spiritual child set out to meet him. As soon as he made a prostration to the Elder, but before he managed to tell the Elder the reason for his visit, Fr Anthimos told him, "Your father is sick. I will pray for him."

A few days later the tumor did disappear and the doctors couldn't believe their eyes. They looked at the biopsy, and then looked again to be certain. The young fellow now hastened with secret joy to meet his father's healer once more, and to thank him. Again Fr Anthimos spoke first and told him, "You poor thing, you don't know what you are seeking! Your father had confessed and was ready. Your favor took place, however, so that you would be assured that God lives and hears our petitions. He always inclines 'a favorable ear', because He is an easily sympathetic Father, and is very merciful and very compassionate.

Later on, the Elder revealed to his young spiritual child his father's age and told him, "Your father got a ten year extension!"

He Will Have a Boy

The craftsman Mr Demetrios Kolentinis arrived at St Anne's during a torrential rain to visit the Elder. As soon as he saw him he felt a huge internal power. The kindly Fr Anthimos told him to change his wet clothes, and they sat at the table. At meal time the visitor told the Elder that his finances were not going well. He was grieving for this, and because God had given him three girls but no boy. The Elder smiled and answered him, "Your finances will improve and you will also have a boy."

He shook his head, however, and said that they did not intend to have another child, because their finances were in a bad state. The Elder repeated his words and said furthermore that the boy would serve the Church. Then he sent him to pray at the miraculous icon of the Entrance of the Theotokos in the church of his Kalyva. He himself retired for prayer in his cell. Exactly one year later, Mr D.K's wife became pregnant and gave birth to a very healthy little boy. Naturally, the family's finances also improved, as Fr Anthimos had foreseen.

His Presence Brings a Good Change

The God-loving couple Euthymios and Helen brought their daughter to meet the Elder and for him to give her appropriate advice. The Elder did his duty and from that day, as her parents attest in writing, the girl realized that something good took place within her for the glory of God, and she felt such power that all her problems were overcome.

He Foresaw Events with Mathematical Precision

On the advice of Fr Anthimos's spiritual child Mr Athanasios Mourmouris, a Customs Secretary, a group of Thessalonians visited him in his Kalyva. The purpose of the visit was to discuss serious topics, and to deliver some of them from the dreadful delusions into which they had fallen. The conversation lasted a while and the Elder explained the correct Hagioritic ideas in detail. The letter which the Elder later received from his spiritual child is worthy of notice. Among other things he mentions, "Things unfolded in the group just as you foretold them with mathematical precision. Except B, who upon hearing your Hagioritic answers which refuted his deluded beliefs received a true discharge of a whole electrical connection. Some of the other followers of the visions and whisperings were electrified with intensity analogous to the level of their delusion. I admit that I also met one with an opposing view, who disagreed with the rest for a time, resulting in them placing him off to the side. He felt joy as soon as I told him the truths I gathered from the Holy Mountain. He thanked me and blessed me at the same time, because divine providence led me to you on the Holy Mountain, in time to prevent dreadful spiritual slips in my later life."

He Didn't Want the Photograph to Come Out

The dentist Mr I.K. from Volos visited the Elder at St Anne's. His wife had a problem and she miscarried a fetus in the first months of her pregnancy. The Elder blessed him and foretold the birth of his child. He was so happy that he didn't know how to show his joy upon hearing this pleasant news. He simply had to have a photograph of the Elder in order to remember him. The Elder didn't want to come out in a photograph, but in the end he was persuaded. However, see what the result was, as the dentist himself describes:

"The God-seeing Elder Anthimos didn't want me to take his picture, but we convinced him to agree. The shot is in the film that I developed, but the Elder doesn't appear anywhere. I believe that if he wanted to come out in the picture, his image would be on the film. All the other shots came out very well. It is amazing that only the shot with the Elder was overexposed. Perhaps the film was burned by the brilliance of his face, the divine light which surrounded him."

The dentist closed his letter with a pleasant event for him:

"We are expecting a child! This is what the Elder foretold. It is a boy, from what the doctors told us. We will name him Nikephoros, because this fetus defeated death, in other words miscarriage."

He Had Little Tumors Which Never Developed

The Elder had little tumors all over his body. Biological tests showed that they were epithelium neoplasms, or carcinomas, which never developed to create problems for him. Thus our God "Who rules over life and death," wanted the Elder to live and to guide many to repentance and salvation. Among other things, the report of histological tests from the laboratory of Anatomy of the "Annunciation" clinic of Athens dated November14, 1947 states:

"It is noteworthy however, that the sufferer, as he himself mentions, had the little tumors for decades, which of course does not agree with the diagnosis of the carcinoma."

A Lesson in the Anatomy of the Mouth

Mr Demetrios Vasileiou relates:

"Three pilgrims were going up from New Skete to St Anne's. One was a dental technician who was studying the anatomy of the mouth at that time. He was telling his fellow travelers that he believed in God on the one hand, but not in the existence of charismatic Elders in our day. The blessed fellow couldn't understand that God's grace dwells within people of our Church and sanctifies them, while those grace-filled and deified bits of dust are the Lord himself "extended unto the ages."

We arrived at Elder Anthimos's Kalyva and received the traditional treat from his disciple. Fr Anthimos appeared and was shining so much that it was impossible for us to look at his face. He embraced us and sat next to us. He began speaking wise words to each one of us. He took hold of our friend the dental technician's face, and began doing the anatomy of the mouth. He was telling him precisely, as he himself admitted later on, the things he had recently been taught in much detail. When the lesson finished, he turned with amazement and told us, 'Now I believe that enlightened Elders also exist in our day!'.

It Wasn't Raining on the Spot Where They Were Working

Father Cyril from the Brotherhood of the Voliotes at St Anne's tells of a miracle which happened when they were repairing the roof of Elder Anthimos's Kalyva of the Entrance. They had uncovered the roof, when suddenly the weather turned bad and the clouds covered the sky of their Skete. A storm seemed to be approaching. Fr Anthimos calmly went to the church of the Entrance, took the icon of the three-year-old Daughter, and made the Sign of the Cross over the horizon. Soon the rain started falling violently all around the Kalyva. Not a drop fell on the spot where they were working, however. Fr Anthimos's prayer had been heard and his boldness before the Lady Theotokos was apparent to everyone.

His Breath Was Fragrant and He Shone Brilliantly

Father John of the Monastery of St Savvas of Jerusalem, before following the monastic way of life, visited Elder Anthimos, to obtain his advice on spiritual matters. He received him with his customary kindness and love. During the conversation, as Fr John told us, he observed that the Elder's head shone brilliantly, and his mouth was producing an ineffable fragrance. He was more astonished, however, when at the end, Fr Anthimos foreseeing his monastic calling, called his disciple and told him, 'Bring a cassock for the young man!'

He Solves a Notary's Problem

The Elder was discussing a specific law with a certain Notary Public. He was interested in the hesychasterion of the Archangels in Vyrona, and had the opposite viewpoint from that which was offered by the notary. At a certain moment the Elder got up and told him, "Go to volume so and so of the penal code, and on such and such a page you will find all that I assert will be unraveled."

It should be noted that the Elder had never dealt with these kinds of matters. He simply had God's illumination and his lips were moved by the Spirit. The next day the Notary found that all the things the Elder had said were corroborated.

Is Father Agapios here?

After the Elder's repose, a pilgrim knocked on the door of the Kalyva of the Entrance and asked his disciple, "Is Fr Agapios here?"

The disciple informed him that there had never been a monk there by the name of Agapios, and that their late Elder was called Anthimos. Then the pilgrim said, "I'm looking for him. I got his name mixed up, because he was the personification of love. He spoke to everyone with vast love and kindness. What a pity that the Anthimos of love has reposed."

After the Vigils He Left Running

The Fathers of the Skete relate:

"Elder Anthimos's Kalyva of the Entrance is above the Kyriakon of St Anne, and there are many uneven steps leading uphill. The Elder, who in his last years was weighed down with the burden of his age, had to stop often in order to climb them. When the vigils in the Kyriakon would finish, however, we would see him leave running and the stairs did not bother him. The strength he would get and the joy he would feel, despite the toil of the vigil, gave wings to his feet, and he went up the steps like a little child, or rather he flew like an eagle, since according to the Psalm he had been «renewed like an eagle»" (Ps. 102/103:5).

Stop Digging and Leave

Fr Clement, an elderly monk of the Kalyva of the Nativity of the Theotokos, which is directly below the Kalyva of Fr Anthimos, relates:

"There is a huge rock outside the wooden fence of my yard. One afternoon I was digging next to it to find dirt for planting a rose bush. Elder Anthimos, who happened to be passing by there, greeted me and told me, 'Stop collecting dirt and leave.'

I obeyed and left without knowing why. The next day, in the morning, I saw that a large piece of the rock had broken off and had fallen on the spot where I was collecting the dirt. Then I realized why the prescient Elder had told me to leave as quickly as possible. He foresaw the rock's fall and wanted to protect me."

Put the Little Paper in your Pocket

Fr Lazarus from Orphanio, Kavala of the diocese of Eleutheroupolis, had written his sins and his passionate thoughts on a piece of paper and went to confess them to Elder Anthimos. As soon as he saw the penitent taking out the little paper he told him, "Put the little paper in your pocket. It's not necessary."

Then he began to enumerate the sins which burdened Fr Lazarus, analyzing and healing each of the passionate thoughts which the humble and pious Levite had written on the paper. He did not omit anything. The sins and passionate thoughts of Fr Lazarus, which had been written down on the little paper, had simultaneously been underlined also in the heavenly report, which the great Fr Anthimos could read in a mystical way.

He Was Fragrant, Like the Relic of St Anne

Fr Maximos who is practicing asceticism at Katounakia of the Holy Mountain, and who had studied Physics told us the following:

"For a period of time before becoming a monk, I had many temptations. Elder Anthimos, who was my Spiritual Father and who knew the tactics of the devil, urged me to be patient, telling me, 'Be patient and God will reward you and will give you many good things.'

"The temptation, however, would not subside and the Elder repeated the same words every time. However, since this happened many times, I was shaken and I thought: If the Elder is a man of God he will reveal something to me. This time, with deep pain, I approached the Elder, who for the first time received me with excessive joy and, when I went to kiss his hand, it was fragrant like the relic of St Anne which is preserved at the Kyriakon of the Skete. I left it and grasped it again and then the fragrance was more intense. He told me with much grace, 'My child, have trust in God and what you want will happen quickly.'

"Indeed, the temptation stopped from that moment.

"The years rolled by and the Elder, like every mortal, departed for the heavenly homeland. The Elder's disciple, Fr Cherubim, asked me to write a few words about the Elder's life for him to read at his forty day memorial. However, I had less than two days at my disposal, and I suffered because of the constraints of time. It was already six in the afternoon but I called the Elder to mind, calmed down and did obedience. I left for Katounakia running. With much satisfaction I wanted to make a deposition, a beautiful testimonial of the Elder's life, but the time was short. At eight at night I woke up to write. My hand wouldn't move until nine. Then I called upon the Elder and asked his help. In ten minutes my mind cleared up and I began to write. In a half an hour I had filled three pages. I read it again, and I liked it. Again I said, 'Elder, is this any good?'

Then a fragrance came to me, similar to that which I had felt earlier when I kissed his hand, the fragrance of the relic of St Anne. The Elder approves, I said to myself."

Curing a Sick Person
With an Orange

Fr Euthymios was the Elder at the Kalyva of St Seraphim, and later went to Esphigmenou. Fr Seraphim, who was the Elder before him, once became gravely ill. He was in unbearable pain and become cynical. Fr Anthimos visited him and gave him an orange from the orange tree at his Kalyva and told him to eat it and he would become well. He also prayed fervently for the sick monk, who quickly felt better. Furthermore, out of gratitude to his Elder, he gave the most precious thing he had in his Kalyva: a piece of the Holy Belt of the Theotokos. You see, Fr Anthimos's prayer was heard by our Lord Who "inclines a favorable ear." The Elder was pure, and God, Who "does not turn away from the filth of the body, but from the impurity of soul," heard his prayer which came from a pure soul undefiled by greed and avarice.

The Bells Rang by Themselves

St Savvas of Kalymnos was an ascetic at St Anne's. He learned iconography from his Elders at Fr Anthimos's Kalyva of the Entrance. When the Saint appeared after his repose to Bishop Isidore of Kalymnos, and ordered him to uncover his holy relics, Elder Anthimos arrived on the island accompanied by four other Fathers. He did not know the monastery of All Saints where St Savvas had practiced asceticism. He was led to it by an ineffable fragrance which drew him to the grace-filled Saint like a magnet. When he reached the monastery after a tiring, uphill journey, the bells began ringing by themselves to welcome him. St Savvas rejoiced that he saw the Hagiorite Elder Anthimos, his successor in exhausting ascetical labors, in his monastery. Astonished by this wondrous event, and filled with gladness and exultation, promised to paint an icon of St Savvas in natural proportions, a vow which he immediately fulfilled.

Dismiss the Housekeeper

A pious doctor from Kavala suggested to his friend Mr E. M., a representative of a large pharmaceutical company in Thessalonica, that he should visit Elder Anthimos and go to Confession. Indeed, he followed his advice and visited him at St Anne's. When he was taken care of spiritually, and before departing, he heard the Elder tell him that his father must dismiss the foreign house helper he had, so that his honor could be saved. It should be noted that during Confession he had not said anything to the Elder about his father. Mr E.M. obeyed the Elder's prophetic words and dismissed the housekeeper upon his return to Thessalonica. He determined that had she remained a little longer, she would have done harm to his father's honor and soul.

Let Her Wait until
She Is Twenty-five

Mr Demetrios Patsias, the Elder's spiritual child from Kouvara, Agrinio, related the following events:

From left to right:
1. Elder Anthimos as a novice (left) with his Elder Fr. Gabriel Lambis (seated) and his spiritual brother.
   Fr. Theophilos Ladas (right).
2. One of the Elder's most recent photos.
3. The Elder's cell in the Skete.
4. Saint Anne's Skete.

From left to right:
1. Elder Anthimos
as a young priest.
2. Elder's holy relics,
to be found inside the Chapel
Presentation of the Theotokos,
within Saint Anne's Skete.
3. The Elder's blessing
at his cell's entry.
4. Faithful waiting for his
blessing on a trip outside
the Holy Mountain.

"Together with two friends we visited Fr Anthimos for spiritual reasons. One of my two friends held a letter which had been handed to him by a young girl who sought the Elder's advice for her future. As soon as he approached him, and before mentioning the case to him, he heard the Elder discreetly tell him, 'Tell the girl to wait until she is twenty-five!' My friend was stunned and was moved by the Elder's gift of discernment and clairvoyance. After a time he informed us that this girl got married at the age of twenty-five, just as Fr Anthimos had foreseen. Furthermore, she was found worthy to become the wife of a priest."

The Wondrous Elder Paisios Kissed His Feet

Elder Anthimos once ended up at Karyes. Deferring to his disciple, he decided to disturb the quiet of the heavenly ascetic Fr Paisios. He went down very slowly to the Kalyva of Panagouda, and with anxiety he rang the little bell in his yard. As soon as Fr Paisios came face to face with the Elder, he not only made a prostration, but also bowed down and kissed his feet, just as he did to every priest who approached him. One saint embraced the sanctified feet of the other. Before the humble cell of Panagouda occurred singular moments of the triumph of humility, which raises us to the heights. Later on, both God-bearing men sat down on the poor benches inside the Kalyva to exchange opinions on various spiritual topics. Before departing, Fr Anthimos, as a priest, blessed the kneeling Elder of virtue Paisios, and the one wished the other, "Good Paradise!"

You Will Become a Monk

The monk Arsenios Gregoriates the Younger related the following event to us:

"Before making the decision to become a monk, I went to Fr Anthimos to confess. When he read the prayer of forgiveness over me, he told me that I would become a monk, to what monastery I would go, and who would be my Elder. I was surprised then, because at that time I didn't have any thought about my dedication. What impressed me, simultaneously with his prophecy, was that during Confession the Elder was fragrant like a spring garden. God's grace, you see, overshadowed him and presented him to me precisely as he was, that is, 'a fragrance of Christ'" (2 Cor. 2:15).

Elder Anthimos Reads us All

The vigils at the Kyriakon of the Skete of St Anne were and are always very compunctionate. In one of these melodious chanters united earth with heaven. Fr Anthimos, standing always in his stall, enjoyed the compunctionate atmosphere and was mentally transported to the divine habitations, where "the pure sound of those who celebrate" ceaselessly glorifies the Lord of glory. Directly across from him sat Hieromonk Philip of the Brotherhood of the Thomades, who chanted with his honey-dripping tone. When he finished a slow chant, he cried out so that everyone could hear, "Elder Anthimos reads us all!".

He was referring, naturally, to the clairvoyant gift of the Elder, who, despite his age, stood as motionless as a statue at his stall preparing to receive "the only sinless Lord, Who takes away the sins of the world."

From His Cell a Heavenly Chanting Could Be Heard

The monk Gabriel, who previously had been the Elder's disciple, who became a monk of Esphigmenou, heard heavenly chanting coming from his cell many times. This particularly impressed him, for he knew well that the Elder never had a radio. However, the Saints and Angels, whom he particularly loved, gave a mystical concert in which the humble ascetic also participated with unceasing prayer of the heart.

He Took Blankets to Put Out a Fire

Fr Barlaam, a hieromonk of the Kalyva of St George at New Skete, saw wondrous signs when Fr Anthimos was liturgizing. Once at the time of the transformation of the precious Gifts he saw the Elder wrapped in flames and instinctively ran and got blankets and towels with which to wrap him. Only when "his eyes were opened" (Luke 24:31) did he step back and cross himself.

Mrs Georgakopoulos from Argos also relates a similar event. She saw the Elder liturgizing, suffused with divine light from the uncreated light, which only the pure in heart can enjoy.

He Was not Standing On the Ground

The bodiless Angels, free from the burden of our clay flesh, have the possibility of standing in mid-air. People are deprived of this ability. The Elder Anthimos, however, as an equal of the angels, seemed to many to be in mid-air and not standing on the ground. Mr Emmanuel Kokkinos, the owner of a restaurant and hotel in Ouranoupolis, also saw him in this way before the door of his Kalyva.

Mr Hercules Georgiadis of Thessalonica saw a similar sight at the Kyriakon of St Anne. Furthermore, he not only saw him not standing on the ground, but saw him shining with light, producing sparks and shining like gold in the sun. You see, the Elder was gold of precious virtue, and by his radiance he dazzled everyone who was in the murky fog of apostasy from the will of God.

Healing with Louiza

Mr Basil Toulikas, the Pyragos from Thessalonica, visited Elder Anthimos together with a certain friend of his. In the conversation they had beneath the porch of the yard of his Kalyva, the Elder revealed several of the problems which were troubling them. They were dumbfounded when they heard their problems being enumerated. Taking courage, they admitted that one suffered with his heart, and the other with his stomach. The Elder knew one medicine for all illnesses, and that was prayer. He prayed for them and his prayer was heard. Then he cut a little branch of louiza (lemon verbena) from a pot which he found before him and gave it to them.

"Take it,' he told them, "and you will become well." The two friends were startled. "One branch of a plant for all illnesses," they said to themselves! They never took into account the boldness of the praying Elder. When, after a brief period of time, they saw the louiza's healing effect on their illnesses, they understood the power of the Elder's prayer to the Physician of souls and bodies, our Deliverer and God.

His Soul Flew to Heaven
Like an All-white Dove

Mrs Angeliki Papazani from Peristeri knew the Elder for many years. She had a spiritual bond with him and humbly obeyed his counsels and suggestions. The last time she saw him at the Metochion of the Archangels in Vyrona she had an overwhelming desire to cover his precious feet with kisses, as Kassiani states in her splendid hymn about the Lord and the sinful woman.

In her daily prayers she first entreated the Lord for the Elder, and then for all the others:

"Among the first, remember O Lord, my Spiritual Father, Hieromonk Anthimos."

On the morning of June 28, 1996 Angeliki got up at four in the morning as was her custom, lit a candle before the icons and began her early morning prayer. Suddenly, in her little room she saw an all-white dove flying and trying to find an opening to leave. She was stunned, because she never had doves in her house, nor could she remember anyone in the neighborhood who raised such birds. Then she remained looking at the fluttering of the little bird of peace. In a little while the dove went to the skylight, tried to rush through, but was wounded by the narrowness of the area, until it found the exit which led to the open sky. It left behind it, however, a few reddish traces of its endeavor for freedom. Angeliki made the Sign of the Cross and continued her prayer, which was disrupted, however, by the question: How was this dove found inside her house in the black dawn? Around seven o clock she set out for the church, and the telephone rang persistently upon her return. It was Eldress Taxiarchia from Vyrona. With a doleful voice she told her that after a little incident, Elder Anthimos left for the eternal journey, for unending blessedness.

At the end of the telephone line Mrs Angeliki remained astonished. "The Elder flew to heaven," she said softly. She thought that the dove was the snow-white soul of the Elder himself, coming to bid her farewell! Its small wound at the skylight signified his fall in the garden and his little incident before spreading his wings to fly freely toward the divine habitations. She began to weep.

IV.
Practical Paternal Counsels

Let Us Not
Commemorate Him

A young lad committed suicide. His crushed relatives addressed themselves to the Elder with the request that he commemorate him, so that his soul might find mercy. The Elder replied strictly, but also wisely:

"Let us not commemorate him in the Liturgy. It is better for his soul. When the most merciful One sees that we are not honoring him, He Himself will have mercy on him, whereas, when we honor him, He will not have mercy on him. Furthermore the others must avoid his example seeing that the Church also doesn't accept him even dead, since suicide is tantamount with blasphemy against the Holy Spirit, which remains unforgiven according to the word of our Lord: "Wherefore I say unto you, All manner of sin and blasphemy shall be forgiven unto men: but the blasphemy against the Holy Ghost shall not be forgiven unto men. And whosoever speaketh a word against the Son of man, it shall be forgiven him: but whosoever speaketh against the Holy Spirit, it shall not be forgiven him, neither in this world, nor in the world to come (Matt. 12:31).'"

Have Children

"Always have great patience during life's difficulties. We can't do anything on our own. The Lord Himself assures us of this saying, 'without me you are not able to do anything' (John 15:6). We are instruments of God dependent on Him. Just as, when we want something, we ask God to give it to us, so also, when He wants to give us something we must take it and thank Him. Don't protect yourselves, but have children. Thus you will show your trust in God, who of course will reward your toils.

Your Husband Celebrates Today

Mrs. Helen Papada took sweets and went to the hermitage of Vyrona to treat Elder Anthimos for her husband's Name Day. It was the Prophet Elias (July 20) on the new calendar. The Elder took it and reluctantly conveyed his good wishes. In thirteen days, however, he visited her house and handed her antidoron from the Divine Liturgy which he had performed that day.

"Today is the Prophet Elias!" he told her and he congratulated her from his heart. You see, he was a genuine Hagiorite, without fanaticism, but with a correct ecclesiastical outlook.

God also Makes
the Water Milk

"You have osteoporosis, the doctors told one of their patients. Drink lots of milk!"
This pious soul asked the Elder to allow her to drink milk during Great Lent, and he replied,

"Don't you think God can also make the water calcium and milk?"

Thus, with his blessing, she did not break the fast and her condition did not get worse.

You Come to Me,
the Simple and Illiterate One?

Certain young people who were comforted spiritually by Fr Epiphanios, the unerring guide of souls, went to seek Fr Anthimos's advice on a serious personal matter. He discreetly asked them which Spiritual Father they had and, when he learned that they were directed by Fr Epiphanios, he told them with a smile, "You have a holy and wise Spiritual Father. You have the source of grace, and yet you come to me, the simple and illiterate one?"

The Fetus is Your Child

The Elder foreknew sins even before those who approached him confessed them.

A young fellow once asked to go to Confession. Fr Anthimos shook his head and told him, "You allowed your wife to have an abortion. You are equally guilty of murder, the murder of your child. How will you, a child-killer, face him in heaven when he calls you 'Father'?"

Sin Causes
Psychological Upheavals

A young lad shut himself up in his house and was overcome with melancholy. His mother was troubled. She ran to Fr Anthimos, to the Hermitage of the Archangels, and gave him her child's clothing to bless. When she explained the case to the Elder, he calmly told her, "The child sinned and sin brings melancholy and psychological upheavals. The 'wages of sin is death' (Romans 6:13). Have him stop sinning and he will recover right away."

Preparation for Death

To the question of how we must prepare better for death, the Elder answered:

"We must prepare, so that we do not die. There is a saying, 'If you die before you die, you will not die when you die.' Our preparation, which should be done in all of our life, is comprised in the following four points:

"Let us constantly die to sin.

"Let us not take courage in whatever good we did to ourselves and praise ourselves.

"No matter how much we have transgressed, let us not despair, and let us know that God allows us to sin so that we can humble ourselves. Otherwise, we cannot enter into the Kingdom of the heavens."

Love for Orphans

Father Anthimos was orphaned from his mother first and then from his father in a very young age. The deprivations, the afflictions, the lack of motherly tender care and family warmth had marked his sensitive heart. For this reason, as much as he could, he showed excessive sympathy to orphans. When once he learned that in Leivadia there was the "Tabitha" orphanage which gathered orphans and made up for the lack of a family roof with Christ's love, he was very deeply moved. What could the poor Anthimos offer? He himself was a lover of "poverty in Christ" and did not have money. He could give his love and his ceaseless prayer to our Lord, the protector of the orphans and the indigent. However, he wanted to accompany his love with something tangible. His handicraft was iconography. He thought, I will make an icon and send them an icon of the charitable St Tabitha (October 25), the saint of Joppa, who was full of works and charities (Acts 9:37). This icon caused particular joy to the orphans, and adorns the small church of the orphanage to this day.

To What the Cenobitic Monk Must Pay Attention

"Two things which are close to the other things, I consider more necessary for cenobitics," the Elder used to say, "obedience to the Elder and to older brethren, and humility, which proceeds from the heart and changes man's old disposition. You will gain the Kingdom of Heaven 'as children of obedience' (1 Peter 1:14) and of humility."

Why Do You Condemn Me?

Serious bad weather forced Elder Anthimos to spend the night at the Gregoriou Monastery. The Fathers of the monastery did not lose the opportunity to gather in the Synodikon with the blessing of their Abbot and to hear the wisdom-filled words of the aged Elder. That which impressed the Fathers more, however, was his obedience to whatever they asked him. He would always reply, "May it be blessed."

They would ask him, "Perhaps we have tired you, Elder?"

And he would reply, "Forgive me, for I have troubled you with my presence."

They thanked him for his soul-benefiting words and he answered them sincerely and spontaneously, "Forgive me, Fathers, for my foolishness and my audacity."

They put him to sit in the abbot's chair of the Synodikon. He was obedient, but humbly and in a low voice asked them, "Fathers, why do you condemn me?"

Our Behavior toward Our Fellow Men Will Save Us

"Our salvation is primarily a work of the good pleasure of God. He wants 'all people to be saved and come to the knowledge of truth' (2 Timothy 3:7). God is not biased. He has mercy on everyone, but he saves the faithful Orthodox Christians, because they have the true baptism and the true teaching. If we want our salvation, we must keep the commandments of God, which clearly state that we must love God and man. The Gospel says, 'If you say, O man, that you love God whom you don't see, and hate your brother whom you see, you are a liar' (1 John 4:20).

"So our salvation depends on the attitude we will take toward other people."

How We Must Pray

"Prayer," the Elder used to say, "means communication directly with God. The Psalmist says: 'I will pour out my petition before Him, I will declare my affliction before Him'(Ps. 141/142:2).

"Before prayer, concentration and a humble disposition and necessary, in other words, in whatever we do, when we ask our superior for help, aid, or understanding of our problems. Through prayer we are delivered from passionate thoughts and fantasies. Fantasy is a deception of the intellect. Man is defiled by the five familiar physical senses and the five senses of the soul, which according to St Photios the Great (Feb. 6) are: intellectualizing, fantasy, amazement, surprise and judgment. With prayer first the intellect is cleansed from evil thoughts and then the heart from its wicked feelings of. For this reason, in the beginning when the intelligible enemy attacks man, first he attacks his intellect, whereas his heart remains undisturbed. Thus, the intellect is easily defiled and easily cleansed, whereas the heart is defiled with difficulty and cleansed with difficulty. To obtain a pure heart and pure prayer is a very difficult work and is identified with dispassion. 'Blessed are the pure in heart, for they shall see God', the God-man Jesus said. (Matt. 5:8). For this reason only the pure are dispassionate and only the dispassionate are granted to see God and His mysteries."

Like is United with Like

The Elder used to say, "Obedience lifts us up to heaven, because it casts off the disobedience of the first-created people. It casts off haughtiness, self-satisfaction and likens us to God. Let us struggle to ascend to the 'likeness,' because like is united with like. Let us unite with the source of light, of virtue and of goodness, Who is Jesus Christ Himself."

Why We Celebrate the Memory of the Saints

"We celebrate the memory of our Saints every year in order to receive strength, to renew ourselves in soul and to follow their example, to the degree that it is humanly possible, of course. They stand by us; they tolerate our weaknesses and intercede for our salvation. Imitating the Saints does not mean obligatorily imitating their martyrdom or their supernatural achievements, but their high ideals, their excellent behavior, and their sincere Christ-centered life style. With these we also will ascend to heaven, to concelebrate eternally with them who comprise our living models and our light-givers toward completion and deification 'in Christ.'

How We Can Achieve
Love in Christ

"Listen," the Elder said, "love is the holiest thing that exists in this life. It is Christ Himself. It is He Who loved us to the point of sacrifice. It is He Who sacrificed His life for His friends, just as He has revealed to us:

"No man has greater love than this, that a man should lay down his life for his friends. You are My friends..." (John 15:13-14).

"Let us love one another with this sacrificial love. Love requires force, as it is written in the Gospel concerning the heavenly Kingdom, 'that forceful men seize it' (Matt. 11:12). So, for us, let the beginning and way to God be 'always to drive ourselves.'"

He is Michael,
Who Will Meet the Lord

Mr Michael Kolitsis from Argos, Orestiko relates:

"On one of my visits to the Elder's Kalyva, he came and sat beside me. His face shone brilliantly as he asked me, 'Do you know who Michael is?'

I was surprised by his question, and pointing at my chest with my finger I said, 'It is he.'

'What he?' he asked me again. 'You are pointing to a shirt. I asked you who Michael is.'

Then I lifted my hand up, and pointing to my flesh I said again, 'There, him!'

'What you are pointing to,' the Elder continued, 'is a cell, which lives as long as it accepts food. If it ceases being nourished, it dies, it is destroyed. So, in order for you to learn who Michael is, listen: Do you remember how you played with your friends when you were a small child? Do you remember your childhood years at school, your spats with your parents at High School, your university education etc.? If you remember these things, this is Michael. The flesh which you are showing me is the shirt of the soul. At some point it becomes useless, it becomes old, you throw it away, it rots! The soul remains and continues. This Michael will meet the Lord in the Kingdom of Heaven.'

Teaching with Divine Illumination

"People teach in three ways: according to the teaching of their Fathers, with human wisdom, or, finally, by God's revelation. The first two ways, if they do not agree with the Holy Scripture, are useless and not only unbeneficial, but also harmful for the souls of those taught. The third way, which comes from divine illumination, of course, agrees with the Holy Scripture and is beneficial and soul-nourishing for everyone."

Attention to the Reading

The great attention the Elder had in the Services did not allow anyone to make a mistake in the reading of the passages. One morning during Matins some lay person was reading the Canon of the Beheading of the Forerunner (Aug. 29). A troparion of the Seventh Ode says, "then the all-unchaste daughter danced...," but he read, "then the all-chaste daughter danced." The Elder was disturbed, shot up immediately standing from his stall and corrected the reader before he completed the troparion. He always did the same thing, when he heard mistaken texts saying that this is blasphemy not only to the saint, but to the Lord Himself, who is the final receiver of our prayers, since we ask him daily: "Let my prayer be directed as incense before you" (Ps. 140/141:2).

His Giving Way
Turned Out Well

Elder Anthimos was a man of love. Once, in the first years of his monastic life a fellow brother of his was tempted by the devil and created problems for him. Furthermore, that brother was the nephew of his Elder, the famous Spiritual Father Gabriel Lambi. In order to give way to wrath and to save his fellow brother's soul, but also his own, Fr Anthimos decided to depart from the Kalyva. He prepared his things and set out for the Skete of Kolitsou, which is near Vatopedi. It was there that St Agapios (March 1) practiced asceticism. He was captured by Hagarene pirates, was sold as a slave to people of another religion and managed to become sanctified under the harsh conditions of slavery with humility and forgiveness. This is what Fr Anthimos also implemented.

Elder Gabriel, who saw how much he gave way and Anthimos's sacrifice to abandon the Kalyva so that the souls might become pacified, did not allow him to leave, and instead sent away his tempted fellow brother and nephew, sending him to their Dependency at Vyrona.

He Always Gave a
Good Example

Father Maximos from Katounakia also relates:

"Before the vigil began, I received the Elder's blessing and told him, 'Elder, since you are very aged, it is not absolutely necessary for you to go down to the Kyriakon for the vigils. Sit in your cell and do the Service on your own.'

He wondering at my suggestion, nodded his head and told me, 'You little fool, do you know why I go down? When you see me, an old shell, attending and standing and standing, won't you be moved, and won't you be urged to come to the vigil also and stand up?'

His love for others dictated that he be a model of life, and give a good, practical example. He always identified love with salvation, for this reason he also said, 'Loving others means that I try to lead them to theosis.'

A Defender of Those with Many Children

Mr K.M., the Athos-loving publisher of the magazine "Parents," visited the Elder and asked him to say a few words for him to put in his magazine. The Elder did not refuse, he smiled and told him:

"Write that young couples should keep God's commandments without deviation and have many children. Those who have only two children are transgressors of God's commandment which says 'increase and be multiplied', because they are two individuals and they bring two children in the world. Increase, that is, from zero population. The Lord is clear and His commandments in this case are twofold. First He said increase and then He said be multiplied. So those couples who have more than four children fulfill the first commandment, which is 'increase.' Those who have more than five please God because they fulfill both of His commands, both to 'increase' and to 'multiply.'

So write to them that they should try to fulfill these commands completely, and to receive their whole payment in heaven, as His submissive and obedient children."

He is the Spiritual
Father of the Wilderness

Once, after the change of the Sacred Monastery of Koutloumousiou to a cenobium, Elder Anthimos happened to meet Elder Joseph, now at Vatopedi, and Elder Christodoulos, the Abbot of Koutloumousiou Monastery, whom Elder Anthimos did not know.

Fr Joseph, a disciple of the great hesychast and niptic Fr Joseph the Cave Dweller, was an acquaintance of Fr Anthimos and made the introductions, 'Over here, holy Abbot, is Elder Anthimos, the Spiritual Father of the wilderness!'

V.

Elder Anthimos as seen by his contemporaries

**Metropolitan Christodoulos of Demetriados,
later Archbishop of Athens and of all Greece:**

In a plain monastic tomb, in the poor cemetery behind the Kyriakon of the Athonite Skete of St Anne, literally between heaven and earth, since June 28, 1996 the earthly relics of Elder Anthimos the Spiritual Father rest, one of the rare personalities which the "Garden of the Panagia", the Holy Mountain showed forth in our century. For many years, pilgrims to St Anne's had the precious privilege of visiting Elder Anthimos, who impressed people just by his biblical appearance, at his cell, which resembles an eagle's nest in one of the highest points of the Skete. An inhabitant of Athos for sixty-three years, the blessed Elder resembled some ancient Prophet, and his austere face and his completely white beard captivated you at first glance. The Prophets of Israel, to whom God entrusted His will, must have been somewhat like that, you think. Nevertheless, down deep this Elder was, like all the genuine people of God: all love, all loving care, all fervor for each one who arrived up to his remote habitation. When he would leave the Holy Mountain and come to the "world," he never lost his virginal innocence, that gentle demeanor which puffs up the inquisitiveness and pettiness of "worldly people."

Short of stature and kindly, Elder Papa Anthimos the Spiritual Father had something divine about him. They called him "charismatic" and a "heavenly man." Others said he was "a God-bearing Spiritual Father and wise teacher." Still others called him "the student of the wilderness." The truth is that his many years of ascesis granted him clairvoyance, wisdom and discretion, the fruits of which were his humility, his love and his unpretentious external behavior, all expressive of his lived experience which life in Christ had granted him, which with wondrous diligence he followed all the years of his earthly life. He went to the Holy Mountain at seventeen years of age, before even coming to know the world and its base evils very well. While yet a child without a mustache, a young adolescent urged to spiritual perfection by godly zeal, Constantine Zafeiropoulos set out from his village, Kallianous of Corinthia, having finished the then academy and he set foot on the sanctified place of Athos for the first time, selecting the sacred Skete of St Anne to dwell, that God-protected castle of ascetical Orthodoxy, with its numerous on the one hand, but much-struggling inhabitants.

Longing for the life of asceticism, he arrived at these sacred habitations, urged by that mystical voice which comes from within and prompts man to take great steps toward the summit of theosis. How incomprehensible are (the Lord's) judgments and how unsearchable are His ways (Rom. 11:33). Who can explain these mystical mechanisms which function in the human heart, and suggest to the "foolish and despised of the world" (I Cor. 1:27-28) a way of life which differs so much from that of the many? Who has the power to approach this mystery and to give a convincing answer to the questions which are always vexing, which the phenomenon of departure provokes both awe and scandal in worldly people? No one else but the very person who always opts for the power of the yearning of devotion to live within him, who considers all as refuse before the sight of God, in the captivation of the Beloved One.

In 1930 he took the big step of becoming a monk of St Anne's. The fame of the Skete at that time captivated him. He was enrolled in the Brotherhood of the famous Elder Gabriel of Madyton, who tonsured him a monk and undertook his spiritual guidance. Anthimos remained near this Elder and his blind brother in the flesh, Elder Michael, submitting with the will and power of an angel, serving them with exemplary dedication, humility and obedience. There he came to know the secrets of the unseen spiritual warfare, the close combat of the spirit, the weapons of the spiritual army, the falls and the victories. His spiritual progress shows also from the fact that three years later, that is in 1933, he was ordained a deacon at the Kyriakon of St Anne by the ever-memorable Metropolitan Hierotheos of Militoupolis, who was himself a permanent dweller of the Mountain. Three years later, in 1936, he was ordained as a presbyter by the same Metropolitan. One does not easily become a priest on the Mountain. To be a hieromonk means to serve every day, blessing and sanctifying the brothers. They do not entrust this work to just anyone. The "Papas," as a hieromonk is lovingly called on the Holy Mountain, is a person worthy of respect, trust and enviable. Papa Anthimos managed to become such a person in six years, very quickly surpassing the obstacles in his uphill course and escaping the snares of the devil. With the grace of the priesthood the Elder developed gradually into an experienced guide of souls, to a healer of wounds which sin opens in the soul, into a refuter of the Evil One.

Much later on he was elevated to be a Spiritual Father. Metropolitan Panteleimon (Papageorgiou) of Thessalonica, himself a Hagiorite and lover of monasticism, offered to lay his hands on him. The Spiritual Father on the Holy Mountainis a genuine interpreter of the divine will. Familiar with one's own capability, with the sacred Canons, the Hagioritic decrees, the practical rejection of the temptations of the devil, and also with the weaknesses of the human soul, he is always called not only to comfort the souls from the burden of their iniquities, but also to heal wounds and sores with the olive oil of divine compassion and the wine of spirituality (like the Good Samaritan). Papa Anthimos didn't delay obtaining the name of a famous Elder-Spiritual Father, full of love for God's creature, "the great wound, man." Whoever met him, especially in his latter years, received the impression of a grace-filled Elder with humanity and sweetness, but at the same time he had an attachment to Tradition. He combined fatherhood with discretion in an excellent, skillful manner. He was a wise Elder in every sense of the word. He knew and respected its measure, its limits, its use. For this reason, whoever sought his advice remained satisfied to the utmost. Just as he was judicious, practical and simple in his life, so he was in his words as well. He laughed spontaneously and frowned with meaning. There was nothing pretentious or false in his behavior. He was genuine.

Because he was strict with himself, he acted with leniency to others. In his gaze you distinguished the ascetic of the wilderness, who inhabits the wilderness. Many times his Kalyva became the refuge of sacred souls. Many who were "heavy laden and burdened" found comfort and consolation near him. He spoke from his deified experience, and for this reason his words were strikingly persuasive. When he participated in the sacred Services, you would say he was flying to the heavens. He seemed worn out after every Divine Liturgy. He would be elevated to heaven mind and heart. He considered the saints as Christ's friends and also his own. He spoke to them with simplicity. He had great reverence for the Lady Theotokos. He reached the boundaries of theosis. For this reason also God granted him the gift of foreknowledge. He used it only unto the glory of God and never for his own advantage and glory.

Sometimes he would go to Athens to hear Confessions. The people waited for him and deposited the burdens of their iniquities at his epitrachelion. He bore them without murmuring, for this was his mission. He respected his superiors, the Bishops of the Church, and his Patriarch. There are pictures of him with the ever-memorable Demetrios, and with His All-holiness Bartholomew. His eyes are throwing sparks from inner satisfaction. He was a churchly man.

During my pilgrimage to St Anne's some years ago, he received me at the Kyriakon, with the other Fathers, with abundant love and respect. He suggested that I bless his Cell by my visit. I eagerly did so. He was flying with joy like a simple little old Elder. He spoke about his Kalyva, and he presented his disciple Fr Cherubim to me, he guided me, with boasting in the Lord, to the various rooms of the Kalyva, to the church, the yard, the balcony. He sailed in oceans of happiness as he saw me treasuring the toils of a whole life. There he had worked with his elderly hands for more than fifty years, building, digging, planting, transferring dirt and rocks. His nest was built with the building material of blood and sweat. Who could know that in June of 1996 he would fall from a wall, in his effort, now at 83 years of age, to reach with his hands some edge, to correct it, so that the wound of disorder would not remain unhealed?

His fall was fatal. On June 28, 1996 he reposed at the hospital of Thessalonica, where he was taken after his mortal wound. He returned to his Kalyva dead. His relics had an ineffable beauty. The Elder was sleeping in the coffin, calmly awaiting the Angel's trumpet. He had already finished his course; he had kept his faith, now the reward of the calling from above awaited him. The Skete Community buried him in the cemetery with all the honors. On his tomb is a black wooden cross, and next to him there is a palm tree, a symbol of immortality.

May we have his blessing.

Magazine "Peiraike Ecclesia," page 16, September 1996.

Archimandrite Nicholas Protopapas, now Metropolitan of Phthiotidos:

"When I met Elder Anthimos for the first time at the Kyriakon of the Skete of St Anne after the Divine Liturgy, I thought I had before me a heavenly man. His face shone brilliantly, like the icons of the Saints, and his eyes gave out an indescribable sweetness. I followed him to his cell, where he accepted me with love, and for hours he spoke to me of God and of Orthodoxy. Then I realized what it means to live in the grace of God."

These few but essential words were written by a pilgrim who loved Athos in his diary after his acquaintance with the charismatic Elder Anthimos. By common admission, the blessed Papa Anthimos the Spiritual Father, was a distinguished personality of the Holy Mountain, a charismatic monk, who with the holiness of his life and his deeply thought out teachings carved a bright course in the Garden of the Panagia, which numbers him among the great ecclesiastical and venerable figures of our age. Great ecclesiastical men named him a God-bearing Spiritual Father and wise teacher. These characteristics are not just flattering titles, but express the conscience of the Church, of his fellow ascetic Fathers, and of very numerous pilgrims. Elder Anthimos of St Anne's was one of the last of the old Hagiorites, who in his person gathered the austerity of ascesis, persistence in the monastic tradition and unswerving observance of ecclesiastical order. He expressed the genuine Athonite monastic spirit, which he imparted to his disciples, just as he had received it from his Elder Gabriel.

From the *Prologue* to his book
Elder Anthimos Agiannantis, the Spiritual Father 1913-1996
(Athens, 1996).

Metropolitan Germanos of Eleias:

During the Feast of All Saints (June 9, 1996) I admired Fr Anthimos at the Kyriakon of St Anne during the Vigil of the Voliotes. His body was bent over, but he was upright in character. Aged, with a completely white beard, but also in soul, he shone brilliantly with his sweet smile of holy joy and exultation. Full of light within and without, the ever-memorable one departed for the eternal light of the three-sunned Godhead.

Elder Moses of
the Sacred Skete of Koutloumousiou:

I met Elder Anthimos for the first time around 1972. He was alone, yet he wasn't alone. In other words, he did not have the elements of painful loneliness which tyrannizes many people in the world. He had a degree of seriousness, a certainty and a sobriety. A sobriety well-weighed, studied, philosophized, not repulsive, but combined with his sweet face, gave you the impression of inspiration, of strengthening. He knew what he was saying. He had studied the Book of life, the history of the rocks, of the kalyves, of the Kyriakon, of the cobblestone paths, of his Kalyva of the Entrance of the Theotokos. He spoke with a beautiful accent, with a rich vocabulary, using all the expressions in the vocabulary of our language. He was not rushed and did not delay. He was literal and observed you with his deeply pondering eyes. He would not allow you not to observe him. He did not pressure you, he did not indulge your weaknesses, he knew how to speak. His pure face, his sunken eyes, his usually rosy color, his very white beard, his sewn cap which had taken the shape of his head, his simple thick cassocks, his calloused hands, his somewhat slow movements, his back which had been bent for many years, the dragging of his feet, and especially his words gave you quite a pleasant warmth. You did not find anything foreign and superfluous in him. He revealed his genuineness, his purity, his grace. His face flourished because his heart rejoiced, according to the ancient philosopher. He was a desirable companion, a friendly, loving, caring, dear Father, teaching, but not tiresome, excessive, fanatic or difficult. He had knowledge of the measure, straight, sincere, honest, precise. If at some point he persisted in something, he was certainly justified. We should never remain so unjust as to isolate and strike out the whole story of a life and offering because of an isolated incident. Isn't that so?

He guided us through the photographs of the Elders who preceded him, both those he had met, and those he had not. He spoke with much respect. He spoke of events of the past century, as if they were today's. He mentioned important details to you. What ascesis, what struggles then, what hardships, difficulties and indigence. And we complain today! There was Elder Theophilos of Madyton, over a century old, erudite in music, slept for a bit in a closet, but remained without rest, to work and pray; and his successors, his brothers in the flesh Michael the Blind, Gabriel and the others. Then he spoke of the Fathers of his greatly beloved Skete of the holy Foremother Anne, of which he served as

Dikaios. The Saints, the Bishops, the Elders, the Madytians, the ascetical, the charismatics, the ascetics, the strugglers of the wilderness, the beautifully chirping sparrows of heaven.

For all these he wrote and told me to supervise the beautiful publication. He knew how to honor, to respect, to be grateful. Now we respect him, we honor him, we are grateful to him. Shouldn't it be thus?

When he entered his little chapel he was changed, brighter, more brilliant, more reverend. He had a paschal face. This was a familiar, very beloved place for him. He had lived many hours with it, inside it. He wore his cassock and his epitracheilion with special attention. He brought the precious relics out for us to venerate. He explained to us patiently. He spoke to us with an excellent naturalness about the miracles of the All-Holy Virgin Mary. He loved our All-Holy Virgin Mary. Truly, what Hagiorite does not? He sat at his stall joyous and united with the persons of the Saints, of so many icons. 'From here St Savvas of Kalymnos passed. Here at us he learned iconography,' he would say.

He took us to the old iconography studio where we saw copies of ancient icons, some half-done and some ready, some brushes, colors, and sketches. They were no masterpieces, but they were skillfully made with love, regeneration, and with prayer, with the fear of God. What can you do with technically excellent, modern so-called Byzantine iconographers, when they are not seasoned with incense, the Jesus prayer, prayer, studying the Life of the depicted saint, but with other smoke, songs and expensive prices?

'Here St Savvas learned to paint icons with us,' he said again. 'He who made the first icon of St Nektarios of

Aegina (November 9), of the Holy Bishop of Pentapolis, who was associated with the Elder Joasaph of Caesarea of our Skete,' he later told us. As he spoke, he took us to the trapeza.

We sat at the frugal trapeza and rejoiced in the ascetic's water and biscuit, the salad and fruit, loukoumi and coffee. The questions of our youthful curiosity made him continue speaking. He had a vast memory; he had a beautiful judgment, beautiful also in his rejections, straight, ready, precise and honest. He gave us something as a blessing.

We descended the cobblestone path for the Kyriakon in silence. We wanted to retain, to not lose what we received. 'What a wonderful man,' my friend said moved. We remember him in all our first unforgettable pilgrimage. I went again. I always remembered that first time. That which marks well an acquaintance. I wonder now as I am writing these meager lines how I remember so many things from then. Later on, he spoke to me about the Holy Mountain, which he truly cared for, without big discussions, about death, about his old age, his beloved brotherhood.

Elder Anthimos belongs to the generation of old Hagiorites who had natural grace. They didn't have the quality of our own cheap materials. They went through many things, they lived pain, they carried their cross without murmuring, they forbore isolation, they made fun of despondency. They had and they gave. They did not give loans, they gave spirit, which they had obtained with blood. For this reason they were blessed.

Sacred Skete of Koutloumousiou. June 1997.

Stylianos Papadopoulos, Professor of Patrology of the Theological School of the University of Athens:

When I first met the blessed Fr Anthimos on a footpath of the Skete of St Anne, he did not impress me very much. I remember two things very well, however: the warmth of his voice, and his face, to which I paid a little attention. Both had something unknown for me, something different. We walked a bit on the footpath. It was not just the two of us. One monk who was walking from the footpath greeted Fr Anthimos, addressing him as "Spiritual Father."

We formally took our leave. A few months later I was climbing the uphill footpaths of St Anne's once more. Now, however, the little I had felt from the voice and the face of Fr Anthimos led me directly to his cell, to the Kalyva of the Entrance of the Theotokos. He was alone, for he did not have any disciples at that time.

This visit opened new perspectives for me. I met a very advanced monk, who lived and acquired virtues through the cenobitic Rule, altered somewhat, according to the customs of the Kalyva and Skete. He was a monk who kept his monastic obligations with exceptional strictness. One who had such dedication to God and to his Elder, that he was so greatly inflamed from ascesis, that the love and grace of God radiated from his face. God showed His pleasure in his joyous, bright face. You would say he was becoming a weak mirror in which you could feel something, a speck of God's infinite love. With this face, Fr Anthimos embraced you and offered you love.

My visits were repeated, and my positive impressions were increased. Naturally, my respect for Fr Anthimos, the Spiritual Father, increased at the same time. This respect and

increased admiration was not due to the fact of lineage. Because we quickly became acquainted like people from nearby villages, even like distant relatives. The blessed one explained to me that we had some relationship, which I did not know, because my father, who was born at Bouzi (Kyllini), at the slopes of Zireia, about 600 meters higher than Kalliani, Fr Anthimos's village, had left the area as a young man. There was another link which associated us. My father's brother, the blessed Bishop Gerasimos (Papadopoulos) of Abydos, who taught and was a bishop in America for 45 years (+1995) was associated with and greatly admired Fr Anthimos. He remained there, however, only four years. He introduced Fr Cherubim from America, the current Elder of the Kalyva of the Entrance, to Fr Anthimos.

Always, when I went to St Anne's, I had the blessing of receiving Fr Anthimos's hospitality. I would stay overnight at his Kalyva. We had many hours for conversation. For me this was a treasure. In the first years, when he did not have disciples, we would stay completely alone. It was fortunate that he would not get tired of speaking and answering. When he did have disciples, again he set aside quite a bit of time for me without neglecting his monastic Rule or the daily services in the chapel.

I was greatly impressed by the way he served in the chapel, with simplicity, joy and humble-mindedness. He created for you the feeling of mystery without formality or imposition. It was also impressive that he could chant the long Canons of Matins with their particular form, in general important, in his sweet warm voice, often without having the book open. He had a very strong memory.

His memory was also shown in our theological conversations, which had great importance for me. Furthermore, after discussing spiritual matters, we devoted all our time to the discussion of other theological subjects. I need not mention that it was I who usually asked and posed the topic, and Fr Anthimos answered. His answers became long because frequently I interrupted, and because he developed his replies based on the passages and opinions of the Fathers of the Church.

His level of knowledge of the Fathers and of the *Rudder* of Nikodemos and Agapios was amazing. I certify this, not only because I repeatedly heard him, but also as a Professor of Patrology, a specialist on the Fathers, whom the blessed Elder Anthimos knew better.

I also went and stayed at his Kalyva so that we might discuss very difficult and deep theological topics. He understood the difficulty, but, I admit, he got to to the heart of the matter. He faced it with relative ease and gave a solution based on the Fathers of the Church. He did this more than once. In some cases, I never heard such accurate explanations. He was the person to whom I could pose the thorniest theological questions. He was a person whose answers were consistently authenticated by the Fathers. It is quite well-known that sometimes Roman Catholics and Protestants would visit him for theological conversation. These people were impressed by his theological acuity, but also by his love, which he showed even when he should have been strict and censuring.

Once, puzzled at the breadth of his theological knowledge, I asked how he managed so well. 'I used to read,' he told me. 'Now I have little opportunity. All during the Occupation, when we did not have orders for icons (Fr Anthimos was an iconographer), I read all day long.' Of course, many people read, they forget the Fathers, and moreover they don't understand the depth of the patristic texts. The blessed Fr Anthimos, on the contrary, both possessed a strong memory and prayed a lot for theological understanding of the things he read. For this reason also the result was amazing. Whoever happened to have a discussion with Fr Anthimos remained with the impression that this monk had great school training, in other words, he was educated. Nevertheless, by contemporary standards, he had not studied at all. The Greek school which he completed in his village of Kalliani is tantamount to a six grade Elementary School, and he did not even manage to go to High School. He just barely completed the Greek School, despite his love for letters. But why should this be?

His strict ascesis, his love and patience in the many daily Services which lasted for hours, the unmurmuring care of elderly monks for three whole decades, the laborious manual work and the acceptance of the various humiliations comprised the practical training for Fr Anthimos who was a monk from 1930 and a hieromonk from 1936. But because this practical training he eagerly accepted and implemented with exemplary self-denial, the blessed Fr Anthimos received grace from God, and also attained contemplation. He became what St Gregory the Theologian (January 25) wrote in 380: "action is the stepping stone for contemplation." Because he loved God and people a lot, because he toiled unimaginably and with bitter tears for his spiritual purification, God granted him states of joy and tears of spiritual joy. Every now and then this joy showed on his pure bright face, in his gaze joyous with love, in moments during the Divine Liturgy when he would serve.

It would be a great oversight if, in a humble commemorative volume about the blessed Fr Anthimos, we forgot to include what he himself did, so that the spiritual presence and the ascetical struggles of the monks of St Anne's may be preserved in the memory of generations of people.

At St Anne's, monks difficult to number lived in a cenobitic, ascetical, anchoretic and hesychastic manner. This sacred and remarkable place knows all the forms of monastic life very well, and for this reason it became exemplary from every point of view. It is literally very fortunate that Fr Anthimos, the Spiritual Father grew white and bent over from his ascetic struggles at St Anne's. With his personal ascetic struggles he understood and unraveled the struggles of the monks who came before him. Like a honeybee he sought out the old contestants advanced in virtue, and he carefully listened to all that the deified elderly ascetics related to him about previous ascetical personalities, about hermitages, about the activities of the monks, the association between them, about where and when each one came to St Anne's and when each one reposed. Furthermore, it is a blessed and good thing that this aged elderly Spiritual Father had such a remarkable memory, so he could retain all these things and dictate them to his disciples. So he published the useful and beautiful book *Saint Anne's: The Sacred Altar of the Holy Mountain*. One regrets, however, that the author of *Elder Anthimos* is brief. He did not say everything he knew about recent and contemporary monks of St Anne's. He only said a few epigrammatic, telegraphic things. He mentioned from where each distinguished monk of St Anne's came, and only outlined the type or manner of his ascesis. Nevertheless, with the work of the blessed Spiritual Father Anthimos we have the first contemporary Synaxarion (lives of saints) describing the recent and contemporary personalities of monastic life who settled in the sacred Altar of the Holy Mountain, the Skete of St Anne at such length.

Now, blessed Fr Anthimos, you live and foretaste the unfading glory in Christ with the monks of St Anne's, worthy and very righteous, whose biographies you wrote. But please remember also those of us who remain, Abba, among whom is he who writes these few lines with gratitude.

Pantelis Yiannoulakis, Publisher:

We ate our food at the Kyriakon of the Skete and, while we were eating, I observed an elderly man across from the place where a lay person was sitting. The main characteristic which impressed me was his surprisingly red face. It was so red that you would think it had caught fire! I suppose that he had very sensitive skin, or some strange illness of the skin, or that the sun had burned him very much, or all of these together. From his speech he seemed very cultivated.

185

Despite the fact that I was tired and not in the mood for conversation, he indicated to me that he was interested in conversation and company. He introduced himself as Isidore Mavrogenis, and in the end I discovered that he was a nuclear physicist from America, a Greek who had returned to Greece to spend the rest of his years, but he also intended to travel to various other parts of the world.

He had a great friend with him, who reminded me very much of a mouse, though I don't remember his name. He, however, seemed more like his subordinate than his friend. We spoke for a bit about the history of the monasteries and I was displeased that he was an obvious flatterer of the three monks who were eating with us.

Later on, in the afternoon, we were going up with my friend to find the house of Elder Anthimos. My friend Odysseus told me that this Elder was the holiest person he had ever met. He was also the calmest one, and the monk on the Mountain who was most worthy of love. He told me that unfortunately he could not repeat the things which the Elder had told him whenever he saw him, because he immediately forgot them, and only the emotions remained to him.

When we entered the yard and went to sit down on the bench to wait for Fr Anthimos, I noticed the red fellow and his friend sitting there waiting! It was completely impossible for them to have gotten there first, because we were all alone when we were on our way up. Furthermore, the Father had not told us that there were other people inside. The red fellow told me that they had come by another road that they knew.

At that moment, the door opened and Fr Anthimos came out. A calm, dear priest with pure blue eyes and a large white beard, with the most kind, loving expression I had ever seen, or rather I knew it: St Basil of our childhood years! He looked at everyone wondering and turned towards the red fellow. He spoke with a soft childlike voice, in purist Greek and seemed more like an educated person.

'What is the purpose of your visit?' he asked, turning toward the red fellow.

'Holy Father,' he said with an unctuous tone, 'we heard that you are a living saint, that you speak with the Angels and that you have great wisdom, and so we came to see you and to get your blessing.'

The Elder's blue eyes bulged out, and he became pale.

'Who told you such things? What is all this? I am just an elderly monk and I am none of the things you were saying (He was really trembling!). Sit down to rest, and then please leave and go pray in the church of St Anne. That is the where shrines are to be found. We are only poor monks here.'

He sat down in sorrow on the bench across from me. He looked at me, but I did not say anything. He greeted Odysseus courteously and I stuck next to my guide so that the Elder would not think I was with the red fellow, who began speaking about a bunch of uninteresting things, while Fr Anthimos listened to him in silence.

Then abruptly and unjustifiably, the red fellow and his friend got up to leave, but the Elder motioned with his hand for us to stay. When the others left and we three remained, I introduced myself to the Elder. Though I told him nothing about myself he asked me if I was a writer! I told them that I was trying my best. He asked me if I believed what I wrote on paper, or if I believed that something else was writing "through me" and I was simply the vessel of an external power beyond me. I answered him unhesitatingly that the second was true. He told me that there is only one Author, and He writes all books.

His one hand was trembling very much, probably from Parkinson's disease. His voice was beautiful and so calm, that it almost hypnotized you as you heard it. He spoke like a kind teacher addressing himself to little children and made his voice sing-songy and rhythmical, so that they could better understand what he was saying. Here's something curious. When he spoke, he would stop every now and then and say over and over again, 'Did you understand me?"

I really don't know what happened that afternoon in the paradisic yard of Elder Anthimos, because as Odysseus had also observed, I don't remember almost anything of the hundreds of things which he told me over two or three hours. I remember only, as if in a dream, images and emotions, his sing-song voice and the euphoria and calmness of the whole world.

He did not mention even one of the usual topics of priests' conversations. Whatever he said revealed such great cultivation that if he were outside in the world, I am certain he would be Greece's greatest professor, and would elevate the level of our miserable universities. I remember him speaking of the Trojan war, the descent of the Dorians, the poisoning of Alexander, the Galatians, the wars of Byzantium, about how the swords and the armor of Constantine Paleologos's army glittered, and about how beautiful our Cretan songs are, and also about the Library of Alexandria and its destruction, about Plato and the world of ideas, about the Balkan Wars and about the first man on the moon! I remember him pointing timidly towards the sky and whispering as if he did not want them to hear him, 'Here at night I hear the orbit of the planets!'

Then, I don't know if it really happened or if it was due to my fatigue that day (I say this as a way out), but looking at him I suddenly saw fireworks on his head! I lowered my eyes and could not look at him. Above his head was a colorful spotlight, which rhythmically cast small rays all around! It was a ring of colors, which strongly pulsated and scared me. However, I felt that I should remain calm and keep my head.

For some inexplicable reason we fell at his feet like little children, and I who usually play the wise man and ask questions, had not said even one word. I only wanted to listen to him. He grasped my hand and I felt my own hand very weak and shaking very much. Then I noticed that the shaking of his hand was being imparted to my own also, and our hands shook together. In a little while my whole body was trembling to the rhythm of his hand.

The Elder showed me our hands which were being held, and then pinched the flesh above his hand and said in a long drawn out way:

'Do you see? We are the same! We are one! Look around you. We are one with all things! All the others are lies. Only God exists, and He is love. He is everywhere, and we are one.'

He said this many times, and I felt for the first time that which I really was. A grieving seven- year-old child who met pain and injustice everywhere and now wanted to weep sobbing in the embrace of his grandfather, and for him to relate whatever he saw in the world.

Suddenly my guide and I began truly crying like little children, because we were little children. Suddenly all the despair and affliction I felt disappeared. It seemed there was a small explosion in my chest, and I felt the greatest calmness and comfort I had ever felt.

"For the first time I heard dozens of birds chirping in the garden and saw the colors of the flowers ten times more clearly. I was intoxicated! I don't know how, but I was sweetly intoxicated. The Elder blessed us and gave us many personal counsels on problems which we had not confessed to him.

"I felt that I had a huge burden within me which I did not know that I was carrying, a ten ton anchor in my chest, and this person had taken it from me in some unseen way. He had taken it on himself. I felt a vast comfort, but he seemed sick and was shaking. Despite all this, his face still seemed childlike and his eyes shone with joy. I remember him bidding us farewell at the door, embracing each other and not wanting to leave him alone. The dear priest was alone on the peak of the mountain, listening to the orbits of the planets in the dark nights.

"We departed and I turned to see him for the last time. I saw him standing at the door and blessing us with the Sign of the Cross.

"A little later I sat down intoxicated at the edge of the cliff, embracing a little donkey and was looking at the sea at sunset. Odysseus considered it a fearful blessing that I had seen the 'spotlight' on the head of Papa Anthimos. He constantly asked me to describe it to him, but I told him that my eyes were tired. We looked there at the sun and saw three wide huge golden rays setting out from the sun and penetrating the whole sky. This was not an optical illusion."

Magazine "Third eye,"
vol. 49, pages 34-36, October 1995.

Archimandrite Ignatios,
Abbot of the Sacred Monastery of Dousikou:

"We had the special blessing of meeting Elder Anthimos in October 1987 at the Sacred Monastery of Xenophontos, when its Abbot, the beloved Fr Alexios, very graciously sent for the precious skull of St Bessarion, the founder of our Sacred Monastery, out of piety and love.

"After the Vigil finished he accompanied us with much paternal love and high courtesy to the Monastery of Simonopetra and both his bright angelic face as well as his honey-dripping words, full of wisdom and discernment, remain indelibly in our memory."

Anastasios Apergis, Publisher:

"He left only good memories to his contemporaries, memories of the spirituality and the ethos, the meekness and the patience, the vigilance and the piety, the ascesis and the humility which distinguished him during his whole life, while his life and work speak to and inspire the hearts of those who seek reflection and uplifting, prudence and love. He is truly a precious ark for the people who come."

Hieromonk Ephraim (Kykkotis):

"Once I went to Dionysiou Monastery to confess and to receive the b"Once I went to Dionysiou Monastery to confess

191

and to receive the blessing of the venerable Elder Papa Charalambos, who always comforted me. This time I was greatly troubled by a difficult personal matter. When I finished the Confession, Papa Charalambos indicated that I should certainly see Papa Ephraim at Katounakia and Papa Anthimos, the Spiritual Father at St Anne's. So, I received his blessing and set out first for Katounakia. With difficulty I saw Elder Ephraim, who told me to not fear, because it was a trial and it would pass. He suggested to me only that I say the Jesus Prayer, and this would free me from temptation. Panting, I took the descent for St Anne's. With ineffable longing I went to the aged and holy Elder Anthimos. When I saw him, my joy and emotion were very great. With tears in my eyes I asked to receive his blessing and whispered to him, 'Elder, I want to tell you something!'

"'I know, I know, my child, but don't fear anything. God and the grace of the Lady of the Angels are with you. God is trying you. Don't show the Tempter that you fear him. He can't do anything. He is the most audacious, timid being which exists. Fight him with attention and prayer. Participation in the Mysteries of our Church is our greatest weapon. When we confess and commune of the Body and the Blood of the Savior Christ, we do not fear the attacks of the Adversary.'

"Because of my deep emotion I couldn't speak a word, but the Elder seemed to know my whole problem. So, once he read a prayer over me, he told me, 'God be with you, and behold, you will find another excellent Spiritual Father who will help you. Don't forget that someone who has a fault accuses others in order to hide his own fault, and then their attention is not focused on him. Whoever uses the Jesus

Prayer is opposed by the good-hating demon, but he should not give up. When man has his hope in God, he is safeguarded by divine grace, and the compassion-loving One does not allow him to be overcome by despair. You must believe that God loves you, my child, even if all people reject you.'

"These words of the venerable Elder gave wings to my feet and with feelings of joyful sadness I went down from the sanctified grounds of St Anne's toward the dock of the Skete. Descending at a curve of the shady cobblestone path so difficult to traverse, I heard steps behind me. I stopped to rest and ecstatically saw the holy Bishop Anthony of Siatista approaching me. As I went to get his blessing he told me, 'Don't be sad! God is life and joy. He will settle things. When you go to your homeland, see that you do a prostration before the Archbishop and he will help you, my child. God be with you, and try to preserve the Jesus Prayer in your heart.' So, he was the person whom Elder Anthimos had foreseen, the one who would cross my path and would comfort me!"

VI.
Publications on the Elder's repose

From the Newspaper
Ecclesiastical Struggle

"One more holy patristic personality passed from the shore of the temporal world to the opposite shore of eternity, and was numbered with the Church Triumphant. This refers to Elder Anthimos of St Anne's.

"I met him for the first time when, together with the already reposed Dionysios Batistatos, we visited him in his Kalyva at the Skete of St Anne, where he lived, and he offered us hospitality for two days. His hospitality was like that of Abraham, his love was non-hypocritical. His word poured forth like cool water to everyone who came to hear him, to quench the material-loving fire, and to light the immaterial fire of divine love in their heart.

"We asked to confess and he, full of loving care and love, took us one by one in the chapel of his Kalyva and before the holy icons which he himself painted did an overall Confession, because, as he himself told us, we had referred to transgressions and omissions from our childhood up to that time. This Confession remained in my memory as one of the most important stages of my life. This is because I distinguished in Fr Anthimos that Spiritual

Father who leaned over you to embrace you, all full of love and understanding, to suffer along with you, to weep with you, but also to assure you that your sins were forgiven.

"He showed such trust in my person, that he appointed me to oversee the renewal of the sacred Hermitage of the Holy Archangels in Vyrona, Athens.

"When we went down to Athens, especially on the Feast of the Archangels (November 8), and he liturgized, whoever had the exceptional blessing of meeting him, but also others who heard from those who had met him, hastened to participate in the Divine Liturgy and to hear the simple, because he had not studied theology, but on the other hand very deep theological words from the experience of his ascetical life, which strengthened you in faith and calmed your soul disturbed by the waves of life.

"I remember that for one of the Divine Liturgies during the Feast of the Holy Archangels, I had invited friends, relatives and acquaintances to participate and to meet Elder Anthimos up close. Indeed, very many responded to this invitation. At the end of the Divine Liturgy, everyone received his blessing, and he had something to say to each one. Even now, all of them speak most highly about the holy person of Elder Anthimos.

"Many times Christians have a completely natural longing to see proofs of our faith with their own eyes. Otherwise, their hope weakens and the accounts of miracles of more ancient times are reduced to mythology in their consciousness. The presentation of new manifestations of our faith in the persons of contemporary personalities of holiness, however, gives satisfactory witnesses of our true and living faith. For this reason we also consider it our duty to refer to the memory of Elder Anthimos as a spiritual memorial.

"The blessed Elder Anthimos of St Anne practiced asceticism at the Sacred Skete of St Anne on the Holy Mountain, for sixty-six whole years. He lived the ascetical Rule as few do. He loved 'fasting, vigil, and prayer' with all his soul. In addition to his monastic duties, like a thirsty deer, he studied the Holy Scripture, the Fathers of the Church, even classical authors, to arm his quiver with arrows and to be ready "to defend to everyone who seeks a word" about our Faith. His obedience, one of the virtues of monastic life, was so discrete, that many times he set examples for his subordinates. As a Spiritual Father he had the sense that in his person the parable of the Prodigal son was brought to life, during which the father runs first to embrace the lost sheep, rejoicing at his return.

"As a liturgist of the Most High he was excellent. He liturgized covered with sweat, and when he finished and came out, he seemed immaterial and transfigured by the grace of the Holy Spirit.

"His handicraft, from which they made ends meet, was iconography. He painted many icons with prayer and fasting, for this reason they bring those souls who piously kiss them to contrition.

"Elder Anthimos shone, literally from purity and the chastity of soul and body, for this reason the opinions among the Hagiorite Fathers were complimentary, as for example that he is "wise." So Fr Ephraim of Katounakia named him. The reposed Fr Gerasimos of Little St Anne's named him God-bearing. Fr Paisios told Fr Anthimos's disciple Fr Cherubim to keep notes of everything that he said. As his disciple and successor, Hieromonk Cherubim of St Anne's related to me, "both those of our faith as well as the heterodox, when they saw him for the first time, ascertained that this was really a charismatic person." Subsequently, when three Roman Catholic travelers from Austria once visited the Elder Anthimos, at the indication of another hieromonk, as soon as they saw him they made the Sign of the Cross and began to weep. Then the Elder told his disciple to tell them in their own language, 'He who remains in the teaching of Christ, also has the Father and the Son'(2 John 9).

"In addition to the above-mentioned gifts which divine grace had showered on him, Elder Anthimos was especially firm in dogma, and what was handed down by the Holy Fathers, and in general, in the traditions of the Orthodox Church. For this reason he left as a sacred heritage to his disciples not to deviate from these traditions, even the slightest degree, and to die in these, just as he did.

"This last heritage is for us Orthodox Christians the best memorial to the memory of the venerable Elder Anthimos of St Anne's. May his memory be eternal."

Vlachoyiannis, theologian
"Ecclesiastical Struggle"# 329 (August 1996)

From the Newspaper *Christian*

"The Spiritual Father Papa Anthimos, who lived at his sacred hermitage for about sixty consecutive years, received a multitude of monks and our lay brothers for guidance.

"His Elder, Elder Gabriel, was also the Spiritual Father of our area. His disciple Elder Anthimos succeeded him, just as the Elders of Russia succeeded one another in guiding the people.

"It is truly a rare phenomenon in our age for the spiritual counselor to impart the ethos and the teaching of the holy Fathers to those who approach. Our age has need of this spirit, which the ever-memorable Elder guided by the Holy Spirit freely, experientially.

"Most of the monks who live today on the Holy Mountain, before ending up in some monastic Brotherhood or cenobitic Monastery, stopped by the ascetic hermitage of Fr Anthimos to seek his advice. Elders, monks, hieromonks, Abbots of Monasteries, Priests and Hierarchs, visited 'the Elder of love' in their difficult moments. With manifest love the ascetic, the genuine child of the Spiritual Fathers of the monks of St Anne's, who showed forth, by the grace of God, so many Neomartyrs, dissolved the passions with love, he courageously confessed the truth and forgave fallen man, guiding him to repentance.

"Three days before his repose, he was with us at the all night Vigil of St Anne. It was the Feast of the Sixteen Neomartyrs of St Anne's. He stood up in his Elder's stall until morning. He did not lower the stall, but remained standing at Matins, standing at the Liturgy, a true trainer, an example for us younger monks and priests.

"Honest and sincere in the confession of faith, he always boldly confessed the teaching and the ethos of Orthodoxy. In all his life with prudence, reflection and courage he correctly portioned out the truth, asserting that there is only one Church of Christ, and only the Mysteries of the Orthodox are valid. He condemned the false prophet and deceiver Mohammed along with all the heretics. Through much study, but also illumined by God, he knew all the deceptions of the Monophysites and examined them for those approaching the truth about the God-man.

"Fr Anthimos constitutes the model Elder and guide for our age, neither lukewarm nor overly-burning, not straying to the deceptions to the right, but neither being insensible seeing the insults to the teachings and dogmas of the Church. Throughout his life he achieved what St Gregory the Theologian called 'always an acrobat.'

"A model liturgist, he was a great example for priests in his Divine Liturgy and in his presence before the fearful altar. His way of reading prayers, carefully and piously recalled the 'holiday of silence' of Abba Makarios the Egyptian. The Elders of our venerable Skete, as the pupil of their eye, keep the rubrics during the all night Vigil, which with his presence, with his sweat, and with his blood, our blessed Spiritual Father finally left as a heritage.

"He would speak the truth to listening ears, when he would see encumbered ears, he would calmly keep silence, pursuing love, peace, harmony.

"The simple Elder possessed knowledge of classical education, ancient philosophy to an excellent degree, like a honeybee selecting only the good and rejecting the deceptions of the Twelve-god monstrosity of demons.

"For many years Fr Anthimos served as the presiding, first priest of our sacred Skete. We younger monks enjoyed a living tradition in his person. He was a genuine Hagiorite, a purely ecclesiastical personality, unpretentious, spontaneous, non-hypocritical, stable. We did not hear a tenth of a drachma's worth of deceptions, fantasies, hallucinations or apparitions from his mouth. He was very restrained in spiritual matters of internal and niptic life, an experienced theologian, since he truly knew how to pray. He smiled condescendingly when he heard about the string of prescient, prophetic, clairvoyant people of our age. Sometimes he would also become strict when he would see religion becoming even abused or like a business, as Alexander Papadiamantis also used to say.

Hieromonk Philip. Brotherhood of Thomades,
Little St Anne's Skete on the Holy Mountain.
"Christian"# 505 (July 11,1996)

From the Newspaper
Morning News of Ioannina

"Orthodox ecclesiastical history and the Holy Mountain are always adorned by holy figures. Such a holy figure was the "God-bearing" Elder Anthimos, according to the hymnographer of the Great Church of Christ, Monk

Gerasimos of Little St Anne's, while, according to Elder Ephraim, the great ascetic of Katounakia, he was 'wise.'

"The words of Abba Evagrios the Solitary are applicable to Elder Anthimos. He says, 'A proud soul is a den of thieves, it cannot bear the voice of knowledge.'

"The Elder's whole life was a prayer, a sacrifice, and a ministry. He was distinguished by a fervent love for the world, and he prayed in particular for its problems.

"A Great Athonite, Elder Anthimos was born in 1913 and reposed on June 28, 1996."

Before and after his repose, many people visited the Kalyva. Every pained soul took refuge and found comfort with the Elder. Far from the noise of the world, a visitor would see the Elder's calm face. His gaze and face showed humility and holiness.

"The Elder saw many things, but revealed few.

"For many he predicted events which concerned them and gave them appropriate counsels.

"Thus the Elder, once he left his last counsels to his successors, humbly took the road for eternity."

Melios Eleutherios
Issue "Morning News" June 18, 1997

From the Newspaper
Thessaly of Volos

"A venerable Elder has departed this life at the age of eighty-three, the elderly Fr Anthimos of the Skete of St Anne on the Holy Mountain.

"He had been born in the village Kallianoi of Corinth, and when he was seventeen years of age he went to the Holy Mountain, where he also dedicated his life.

"He was ordained deacon in 1933 by Metropolitan Hierotheos of Militoupolis, and he became a priest in 1936.

"He was a charismatic person, spiritual, and a visionary, with particular interest in the young, whom he always counseled for the better."

Issue of 7.4.1996.

From the Newspaper
Orthodoxos Typos

"On the 28th of the past month Hieromonk Anthimos, the Spiritual Father of the Sacred Skete of St Anne, fell asleep in the Lord at 86 years of age. He spent sixty consecutive years in the above Skete accepting a multitude of monks and lay brothers for guidance. Most monks who live on the Holy Mountain went by the Elder Anthimos's Kalyva to seek his advice before ending up in a monastic Brotherhood. For many years Fr Anthimos served as the one who presided, the first priest of the Sacred Skete, while his Brotherhood enjoyed a living tradition in his person. He was a genuine Hagiorite, a purely ecclesiastical figure who was unpretentious, spontaneous, non-hypocritical, and not deluded. His Brotherhood bears a weighty inheritance, and also the prayer and blessing of a contemporary ascetic and philanthropic Spiritual Father."

Issue 1182, July 19, 1996.

From the *Protaton Magazine*

"The aged Elder Anthimos, the hieromonk the Spiritual Father of St Anne's (1913-1996) of the Kalyva of the Entrance of the Theotokos, of the Theophileon, of the Sacred Skete of St Anne, in the world Constantine Zafeiropoulos, from Kallianoi, Corinth. In 1929 he arrived at this Kalyva, and was tonsured the following year. He was ordained deacon in 1933 and priest in 1936, and he was famed as a discerning Spiritual Father. Many souls were comforted at his epitrachelion. He was an experienced knower of the Hagiorite tradition and history, a person of love, monastic and a lover of good.

VII.
Letters for the publication of his life

THE SACRED MONASTERY OF IVERON, ON THE HOLY MOUNTAIN
September 17/30, 2000

Beloved Fr Cherubim,

We received the book *Elder Anthimos of Saint Anne's* by Mr Charalambos Bousias, which you have published with so much diligence and good taste, as a pious memorial to your venerable Elder of blessed memory, and we fervently thank you for the gracious and brotherly gift.

While we pray our Lord Jesus Christ, through the intercessions of our miracle-working Protectress the Panagia the Keeper of the Portal, and through the prayers of Elder Anthimos, may richly bless your Brotherhood in Christ, guiding it to saving pastures.

With much love in Him,
The Abbot of the Sacred Monastery of Iveron
+ Archimandrite BASIL and my brothers in Christ.

THE SACRED MONASTERY OF GRIGORIOU
February 15/28, 2000

Father Cherubim, bless.

With great and unexpected surprise, I received the book you recently sent to me with honor and piety and thanksgiving, which was published through your care, by the providence and striving of the most pious hymnographer Dr Charalambos Bousias, concerning the Spiritual Father and teacher, the hieromonk Fr Anthimos of Saint Anne's, your godly-wise venerable Elder, who is worthy of blessedness.

We are indebted to you, for you acted well and in a God-pleasing manner to present to the wider Orthodox pleroma the venerable personality of your Elder, adorned by many virtues, whose passing by, even in silence and chastity, created a wondrous impression and taught us through his great simplicity, his utter and godly wisdom in the Holy Spirit, and the courteousness which distinguished him.

I thank you because in this biographical volume which you have published, you included certain excerpts from the blessed Elder's impromptu arrival at the Brotherhood of our Sacred Monastery due to a sea storm, and he set a spiritual table for our holy monastery with various and choice teachings from his honey-flowing mouth for our spiritual nourishment.

In these times which are devoid of high significance, which we are undergoing by the prayers and intercessions of your blessed Elder, may we the least of monks struggle in a God-pleasing way and imitate the saints during these wicked times, hoping to obtain eternal delight and unspeakable blessedness, praying for one another and spiritually standing with one another.

With many thanks for your esteemed gift and your fraternal prayers.

The least among monks,
DAMASCENE GREGORIATIS

THE HOLY MOUNTAIN
August 19, 2000

Very beloved brother in Christ,

I fervently thank you for courteously sending me the very noteworthy and soul-benefiting work of the most pious Mr C. Bousias, *Elder Anthimos Of Saint Anne's*, about the life and the spiritual counsels of the ever-memorable Elder.

I look for the aged Elder's supplications to God, and humbly wish you strength from on high on the path of your monastic life and in your godly occupations and activities.

With many prayers,

The Abbot of the Sacred Monastery of Pantocrator
+ Archimandrite BESSARION

METROPOLITAN EUSTATHIOS OF MONEMBASIA AND SPARTA

My beloved Fr Cherubim,

Please accept my whole-hearted thanks for the precious gift of the bright work of our friend Charalambos Bousias concerning the holy figure of the venerable and truly holy Elder Anthimos.

With respect and embraces,
+ EUSTATHIOS of Monembasia and Sparta

METROPOLITAN NIKODEMOS OF PATRA

Fervent thanks and prayers for your kind gift of the book *Elder Anthimos Of Saint Anne's*. It is praiseworthy to set forth such holy personalities for imitation.

With prayers in the Lord,
+ NIKODEMOS

METROPOLITAN AMBROSE OF
KALAVRYTA AND AIGIALEAS
September 28, 2000

My beloved Father,

With exceeding joy I received *Elder Anthimos Of Saint Anne's*, the work of the most erudite Mr Charalambos Bousias, and I thank you.

It is a very noteworthy, elegant and spiritually beneficial work, because of the author's biographical narrative, as well as for the personal impressions of many spiritual men which are contained in the present volume. It is easily ascertained that the blessed Elder Anthimos of St Anne's was a charismatic, wise teacher, and God-bearing Spiritual Father.

Our century was, by the grace of the Lord, full of such personalities (mentioned in the author's Prologue), who gave their spiritual fragrance and spiritually supported a multitude of questioning souls.

May we have his blessing, and may the Lord also show forth such ascetical and God-bearing personalities during the twenty-first century, which promises to be stormier than the previous one.

With love in the Lord,
+ AMBROSE of Kalavryta and Aigaleas

METROPOLITAN THEOKLITOS OF AITOLIAS AND AKANARNANIAS

With joy we received the book you sent, *Elder Anthimos Of Saint Anne's*, the wise and God-bearing contemporary Father of Athos. Congratulating you from our heart, we thank you for this courteous offering.

May the ever-memorable Elder, who is at the Lord's right hand, pray also for us who are in the world.

With fervent prayers and respect,
+ THEOKLITOS of Aitolias and Akanarnanias

METROPOLITAN JEROME OF THEBES AND LEIVADIA

My beloved Fr Cherubim,

I had the good fortune to meet the Elder and to kiss his hand. I thank you for the book. When I visit the Holy

Mountain, I will come to venerate the tomb of the Elder, that "truly wise God-bearer and Father."

With prayers,
+ JEROME

METROPOLITAN MAXIMOS
OF SERRON AND NIGRITIS

Your excellent book *Elder Anthimos Of Saint Anne's*, which Fr Cherubim, the Elder of the Brotherhood of the Theophileon sent me as a gift, is soul-benefiting and elegant. It vividly presents the light-figured personality of a contemporary Saint, who supported many souls.

Today's world, which smells of filth, needs to receive an example from the holy life of people of such spiritual stature. Elder Anthimos, a hidden treasure, was revealed in your well-written book, so he could become a bright rainbow in the path of many faithful people. The grace of God brings such diamonds and such models to light, no matter how much they hide, so that they may guide His people.

The simple and practical manner with which you present the wise words and the graceful snapshots from the life and the correspondence of the ever-memorable holy

Elder, make your work attractive and edifying. I pray that the Lord may also grant you to write similar soul-benefiting books, and to continue writing your precious spiritual offerings in good health.

With His love,
+ MAXIMOS of Serron and Nigritis

METROPOLITAN PROKOPIOS OF NEA KRINI AND KALAMARIA

I thank you for sending me the book entitled *Elder Anthimos Of Saint Anne's*, and I pray that his venerable example guides every reader of this work in the realization of the ideal, which is the inheritance of eternal life, in which the blessed Elder dwelt.

With prayers,
+ PROKOPIOS of Nea Krini and Kalamaria

METROPOLITAN HIEROTHEOS OF NAFPAKTOS AND SAINT BLASIOS

Beloved Fr Cherubim,

I thank you very fervently for sending me the book about the blessed Elder Anthimos of St Anne's.

I read it and was very moved, because I am attracted to the heremitic-hesychastic monasticism, and also because the ever-memorable Elder had benefited me by his love and kindness, when as a young student I met him at vigils in cells of the wilderness and received his blessing. He loved us very much and manifestly expressed it. I remember his courtesy and his spiritual and joyous speech.

May we have his blessing.
I wish you strength and much patience.

With much love,
+ HIEROTHEOS of Nafpaktos and Saint Blasios

THE SACRED METROPOLIS
OF NEAPOLIS AND STAVROUPOLIS

Beloved Fr Cherubim,

With great joy I received the book published by your Brotherhood, *Elder Anthimos Of Saint Annes's*, which you sent me with love, and I thank you from my heart. The great virtue of gratitude toward our Spiritual Fathers moves me very deeply, and for this reason I sincerely congratulate you. The book, exceptional in itself and also for its content, happened to have a rare author, the wonderful scholar and amazing hymnographer Mr Charalambos Bousias. I congratulate you from my whole soul for everything.

May the prayers of the grace-exuding Fr Anthimos accompany you always, as you also commemorate My Humility in your prayers and supplications.

With prayers and love for all the Brotherhood,
+ DIONYSIOS, Metropolitan of Neapolis and Stavroupolis

METROPOLITAN MELETIOS OF NIKOPOLIS

I thank you fervently for sending the book *Elder Anthimos Of St Anne's*, by Mr Charalambos Bousias.

I had heard many things about this ever-memorable Elder. Now my desire to meet him has been fulfilled.

He was certainly a venerable and true Elder. May he illumine and guide "both young and old" by his example and his inner humble manner.

May you also have his blessing, walk in his footsteps and follow him in his journey above.

With the embrace of love,
+ MELETIOS of Nikopolis

ECUMENICAL PATRIARCHATE,
THE SACRED METROPOLIS OF KOS

We thank you for graciously sending the book by the author Dr Charalambos Bousias *Elder Anthimos Of St Anne's* which traces the whole life on the Holy Mountain of the reposed aged and wise Elder Anthimos, this ascetical personality of the Kalyva of the Entrance of the Theotokos in the Skete of St Anne.

The story of the life of the simple Elder in this book includes many opinions and reflections of venerable personalities, as well as articles from magazines and newspapers. It constitutes the halo of this great ascetic figure, and urges every reader to glorify our Holy God, because during the years of apostasy from His will, He shows forth such figures who are in close communication with our Savior Christ, purifying and sanctifying themselves in order to become pleasing to Him, thereby eliciting people's praise and admiration.

With paternal blessings,
+ AIMILIANOS, Metropolitan of Kos

THE SACRED METROPOLIS OF PETRA

My beloved Fr Cherubim,

I embrace you in Christ and thank you very much for sending the precious book of your beloved Brotherhood concerning the ever-memorable Elder Anthimos.

He was truly charismatic, spiritual and God-loving. He honored our Church. He enriched the Holy Skete with so many spiritual experiences and comforted thousands of people by his loving care and love.

I met him, respected him and heard his discerning counsel, and he honored me with his love.

Congratulations, holy Elder, for the gift which your own Brotherhood now gives in this present work.

Many blessings to all the Fathers, and I do a prostration, asking that you commemorate me because the hierarchal Cross is heavy and there are very few Cyrenians in our days just "as in the days of Noah" (Matt. 24:37).

With prayers and love,
+ NEKTARIOS, Metropolitan of Petra

METROPOLITAN DEMETRIOS
OF GOUMENISIS AXIOUPOLIS AND POLYKASTROS

I received with much pleasure the most wonderful spiritual portrait of your God-bearing Elder Anthimos, the reposed (or rather blessed), the reposed (or rather now living forever) Spiritual Father of attested venerable life and conduct, who in an abundance of love and fervor of heart, vigilantly watches over all his spiritual children and over us, the pious readers of this sacred book.

I confess that this book perhaps constitutes the Christ-loving and saint-loving author's best "poetic" creation. It is simultaneously an excellent school of virtue, of ascetic love of toil, of prayerful persistence, love in holiness, holiness in humble-mindedness, humble-mindedness in love for God, and whole-hearted love for God, and truly exudes a spiritual fragrance. This is because, in obvious humility, the pious author managed to depict, as much as possible, through the results and energies and teachings and miracles, your venerable Elder's hidden life in Christ God to such a degree that each reader can somewhat perceive the brilliance of such a life, and sit rejoicing spiritually at the feet of your venerable Father.

+ DEMETRIOS of Goumenisis

METROPOLITAN ANDREW
OF DRYINOUPOLIS AND POGONIANIS AND
KONITSIS

Beloved Fathers and Brethren,

I greatly thank your Brotherhood and Fr Cherubim for the very beautiful book you sent me. Fr Anthimos was truly an important figure. May God give us such choice figures for the edification of our Holy Church. I pray (that you receive) "every good gift and every perfect gift" from the Lord. Bless.

+ ANDREW of Dryinoupolis

METROPOLITAN CYRIL OF KITHIRON

My beloved Fr Cherubim,

Fervently thanking you for your precious offering of the profound work *Elder Anthimos of Saint Anne's* by Mr Charalambos Bousias, I pray that the prayers of the Elder Anthimos and the contemporary saints of Athos accompany both you and us.

With heartfelt brotherly embraces and love in the Lord,

+ CYRIL of Kithiron

METROPOLITAN SERAPHIM OF STAGON AND METEORON

My beloved Fr Cherubim,

With much joy we received Mr Bousias's book which presents the bright personality of the ever-memorable Elder Anthimos. It is an important offering, since the exceptional Spiritual Father and wise Elder Anthimos left a great spiritual inheritance which must be made known so that it may inspire people.

Your Brotherhood must be glad that this book is in circulation, since thereby the life and work of this chaste Elder, when in silence and prayer he led a multitude of souls to the Savior God, will become known to a wider public.

I pray continuously that your chosen Brotherhood may continue to offer itself with self-denial and love as a model of virtuous and true monastic life in our contemporary world.

My blessings and my love to the Fathers.

With many blessings,
+ SERAPHIM of Stagon and Meteoron

ARCHDIOCESE OF ATHENS,
SACRED MONASTERY OF THE BODILESS POWERS, PETRAKI

My Venerable Elder Fr Cherubim,

"Rejoice in the Lord always."

In this letter, we respectfully desire to express to you our most fervent thanks for sending the work of Dr Charalambos Bousias entitled *Elder Anthimos Of Saint Annes's*, asking that you convey our heartfelt congratulations to the author of the aforementioned work, for his toils and labors in writing this book.

The aforementioned work is very elegant, descriptive, didactic and soul benefiting for the reader. The reader will profit very much from reading the text, and also from the descriptive photographs.

Kissing your right hand with profound respect,

the Abbot
Archimandrite PAUL SP. TSAOUSOGLOU, Hieropreacher

THE SACRED AND VENERABLE CENOBITIC WOMEN'S MONASTERY OF SAINT PATAPIOS, LOUTRAKI

Venerable Elder, bless.

We humbly express our fervent thanks for *Elder Anthimos,* which you sent us as a blessing. Although we live quite far from the Holy Mountain, that truly spirit-bearing man's holy life and progress in God were not unknown to us.

May his blessing strengthen us all, and may our zeal be stirred to imitate his bright example.

With deepest respect,
Nun ISIDORA and my sisters in Christ

SACRED METROPOLIS OF THESSALONICA, THE SACRED WOMEN'S MONASTERY OF THE DORMITION OF THE THEOTOKOS OF PANORAMA

Very respected Elder,

We feel the need to express our deepest thanks and gratitude for the book, "salted with grace" (Col. 4:6), about the blessed Elder Anthimos of St Anne's, which you paternally sent us.

"God is wondrous in His Saints." Delving into its pages truly refreshed us in the Holy Spirit, strengthened our souls, and aroused our longing for virtue.

We humbly pray our Panagia to support you richly in the much toiling, holy pastoral ministry which you perform. We also ask you to pray for our Sisterhood at the Holy Altar.

With deepest respect,

Abbess FEBRONIA and the sisters in Christ with me

KALYMNOS,
THE SACRED MONASTERY OF ALL SAINTS
September 10, 2000

Father Cherubim, rejoice in the Lord.

I pray that you may be always well.

A few days ago I received the book about the blessed Elder Anthimos, and I thank you very much.

I read it with much attention and interest and saw the majesty of the man. He was charismatic and very blessed by God.

You had the honor of having him as your Elder, and of enjoying his spiritual wealth.

The Abbess and the sisters wish you health, joy and every good thing.

With much love,
Archimandrite AUGUSTINE

THESSALONICA

My Venerable Father Cherubim,

I received Mr. Charalambos Bousias's wonderful book *Elder Anthimos of Saint Anne's*, which you sent me. I have already read nearly all of it, and am enjoying it for its elegant tone and its very spiritual content. I pray that many of our brothers reap edification and divine blessings through the prayers of the holy Elder. May we have his blessing, you his direct subordinates, his spiritual children, and all of us who are becoming acquainted with him indirectly, and are being edified by his words and his life, which are printed in the very pious Mr Bousias's book.

I congratulate you on the publication and fervently thank you.

JOHN M. FOUNTOULIS,
Professor at the University of Thessalonica

VIII.
Great Vespers

By Charalambos M. Bousias
Translated by Archimandrite Seraphim Dedes

At, Lord I have cried. **Prosomoia.**
Mode 4. *You have given.*

Glorious St. Anthimos,
you are a treasure of theology,
and the home of all the virtues,
the dwelling of divine grace,
and the purest vessel,
and the bright example
of true obedience in Christ,
and of humility, O blessed one.
By your divinely wise words, you illumined
those sleeping in darkness,
who took refuge in your venerable
way of life and your holiness.

In recent times, you were known
for being zealous about the prize
of perfection attained in Christ,
for being a genuine
model for ascetics,

and a living image
of the inspired priest of God.
Therefore with gladness we celebrate the day
of your all-honored memory,
and we unceasingly call you blessed,
holy Father St. Anthimos,
as one filled with the Spirit's gifts.

You were young, Father Anthimos full of grace,
pearl of understanding and treasure of vigilance,
when you left behind
Corinth's rugged mountains.
When you went to Athos,
the Holy Mountain, there to live,
you decorated it with the gorgeous plants
and flowers of your vigorous ascetic labors, all-lauded one;
and you watered them with the streams
of your copious sweat and tears.

You walked in the footsteps of the ancient Fathers
in recent times.
You were known as a minister
and priest of the Most High God,
for you were transported
by intense divine love.
You were an unerring guide of souls
unto perfection, O Father Anthimos.
Therefore, you were counted worthy to enjoy immortality in
the company of the saints
in the heavens, O blessed one.

O wise one,
as a powerhouse of constant prayer, and a treasure-house
of the knowledge that comes from God,
you shone as the much-admired
jewel of St. Anne's Skete.
Anthimos, you labored
with ardent zeal into old age,
like a teenager filled with zest for life.
You ministered to everybody who came to you with
reverence, requesting your fervent prayers
to the Lord God on their behalf.

By the grace of the Spirit you flourished as a sweet-scented
flower of holy virtue and watchfulness
on Athos, that sacred mount
and delightful garden.
By the godly fragrance
of all the gifts you had from God,
you drove away the offensive smell of our
rebelliousness, O holy man;
and you gave spiritual mirth to all,
with your sweet and divinely wise
words and sayings, O Anthimos.

Glory. Mode pl. 2.

Let us honor that God-bearing and wise Spiritual Father of
Athos, who adhered strictly to the traditions of the Fathers
and to the holy Canons, that father with divine insight, the

ever-venerable Anthimos. He never ceased forcing himself, and thus he ascended to heights of virtue and perfection that are hard to imagine. He conversed with saints, and he was filled with heavenly graces. And now, as he enjoys the delightful flower garden of unending joy and happiness, he intercedes with our God, Christ the King of all, to fill with sweet fragrance the souls of those who celebrate his memory.

Both now. **Theotokion.**

Who would not pronounce you blessed O all-holy Virgin? Who would not sing praises of your childbirth without travail? For the Only-begotten Son Who timelessly shone forth from the Father, did Himself come forth from you O pure one, ineffably incarnate. Since He was God by nature, for us He also became man by nature. He was not thus divided into two persons, but now is rather known in two natures without confusion. To Him pray fervently, O august and all-blessed Maid, that His mercy may come upon our souls.

The Entrance. *Gladsome Light.*
Prokeimenon of the day, and the Readings (NRS).

The reading is from the *Wisdom of Sirach.*
(51:13-25)

While I was still young, before I went on my travels, I sought wisdom openly in my prayer. Before the temple I asked for her, and I will search for her until the end. From the first blossom to the ripening grape my heart delighted in her; my foot walked on the straight path; from my youth I followed her steps. I inclined my ear a little and received her, and I found for myself much instruction. I made progress in her; to him who gives wisdom I will give glory. For I resolved to live according to wisdom, and I was zealous for the good, and I shall never be disappointed. My soul grappled with wisdom, and in my conduct I was strict; I spread out my hands to the heavens, and lamented my ignorance of her. I directed my soul to her, and in purity I found her. With her I gained understanding from the first; therefore I will never be forsaken. My heart was stirred to seek her; therefore I have gained a prize possession. The Lord gave me my tongue as a reward, and I will praise him with it. Draw near to me, you who are uneducated, and lodge in the house of instruction. Why do you say you are lacking in these things, and why do you endure such great thirst? I opened my mouth and said, acquire wisdom for yourselves without money.

The reading is from *Proverbs*.
(3:11-18)

Do not let loyalty and faithfulness forsake you; bind them around your neck, write them on the tablet of your heart. So you will find favor and good repute in the sight of God and of people. Trust in the Lord with all your heart, and do not rely on your own insight. In all your ways acknowledge him, and he will make straight your paths. Do not be wise in your own eyes; fear the Lord, and turn away from evil. It will be a healing for your flesh and refreshment for your body. Honor the Lord with your substance and with the first fruits of all your produce; then your barns will be filled with plenty, and your vats will be bursting with wine. My child, do not despise the Lord 's discipline or be weary of his reproof, for the Lord reproves the one he loves, as a father the son in whom he delights. Happy are those who find wisdom, and those who get understanding, for her income is better than silver, and her revenue better than gold. She is more precious than jewels, and nothing you desire can compare with her. Long life is in her right hand; in her left hand are riches and honor. Her ways are ways of pleasantness, and all her paths are peace. She is a tree of life to those who lay hold of her; those who hold her fast are called happy.

The reading is from the *Wisdom of Solomon*.
(5:15 – 6:3)

But the righteous live forever, and their reward is with the Lord; the Most High takes care of them. Therefore they will receive a glorious crown and a beautiful diadem from the hand of the Lord, because with his right hand he will cover them, and with his arm he will shield them. The Lord will take his zeal as his whole armor, and will arm all creation to repel his enemies; he will put on righteousness as a breastplate, and wear impartial justice as a helmet; he will take holiness as an invincible shield, and sharpen stern wrath for a sword, and creation will join with him to fight against his frenzied foes. Shafts of lightning will fly with true aim, and will leap from the clouds to the target, as from a well-drawn bow, and hailstones full of wrath will be hurled as from a catapult; the water of the sea will rage against them, and rivers will relentlessly overwhelm them; a mighty wind will rise against them, and like a tempest it will winnow them away. Lawlessness will lay waste the whole earth, and evildoing will overturn the thrones of rulers. Listen therefore, O kings, and understand; learn, O judges of the ends of the earth. Give ear, you that rule over multitudes, and boast of many nations. For your dominion was given you from the Lord, and your sovereignty from the Most High.

At the Litia:
Idiomela. Mode 1.

Leap and dance for joy, O Holy Mountain Athos, and celebrate the splendid and solemn memory of your wise son, Anthimos, that newly shining beacon of piety. He depicted in himself the virtues of the God-bearing Fathers of old, and he distinguished himself in vigorous asceticism and sound advice, and he enlightened many people, lay and celibate. Therefore he received the honors of incorruption from the Lord, and with Him he rejoices forevermore, and he unceasingly prays for world peace and the salvation of our souls.

Mode 2.

From the time of your childhood, you dismissed the futility of earthly pleasures, and you strove for what is eternal and incorrupt. Thus you became a tireless worker of virtue, and an ascetic gifted with the wisdom of God, O Anthimos. When you mortified the flesh with its passions and desires, and expelled all wicked thoughts by grace divine, you attained life that never ends. Now that you have put on the imperishable crown, as you rejoice together with the holy

Fathers in the dwellings of the righteous, pray unceasingly to our merciful God, that He grant us forgiveness of sins and great mercy.

Mode 3.

Adorned with the gift of insight, you astounded all with the grace that was given you from heaven, O spirit-bearing Anthimos. Your God-inspired words of wisdom revealed what was in the depths of peoples' hearts; and your refreshing cheerfulness revived the souls of those who came to you. As you now repose in the bosom of Abraham, O blessed one, cease not to pray to Christ, that he revive and refresh us who are enflamed by sin.

Mode 4.

The God-protected village of Kalliani in recent times produced Anthimos the spiritual director of Athos, and his relative Kassiani, the most devout ascetic, like two juicy bunches of grapes from the same root. As we collect the nectar of their labors, let us glorify Christ who has now shown us these His devout servants.

Glory. Mode 4.

Let us sing in praise of Anthimos. He found protection in the loving embrace of our Lady Theotokos, the mother of all orphans. In recent times, by emulating the devout Fathers of old, he shone forth in the monastic life, like a new star, in the

Skete of Saint Anne, the ancestor of God. Now that he is a citizen of heaven, he brings propitiatory prayers to the Lord on our behalf, that we find mercy on Judgment Day.

Both now. **Theotokion.**

Guard your servants from dangers of every kind, O blessed Theotokos, so that we may glorify you the hope of our souls.

At the Aposticha. **Prosomoia.**
Mode pl. 1. *Rejoice.*

Rejoice, scion of Kallianoi,
and sacred gem of the Corinthian prefecture;
the new pride and joy of Athos,
as one whose eminent life
was completely pleasing
to the all-good God.
Intense love of God gave wings
to your heart and your intellect;
you thus transcended
all things base and material,
and you lived your life
emulating the bodiless.
Therefore you hastened to attain
the all-joyous flowerbed,
as well as spiritual glory;
which we entreat you to share with us,
who sing in your honor,
O God-bearing holy Father, all-blessed Anthimos.

Verse: Precious in the sight of the Lord is the death of His saint.

Rejoice, O Saint who from a young age
were fond of stillness and the spiritual way of life.
The devout Fathers of Mount Athos
considered you their most prized
ornament and jewel,
Anthimos most wise.
The resident of the Skete
of St. Anne the forebear of God,
you saw the future
and foretold what would come to pass;
and to all who came to you seeking your help you gave
cures for their soul's infirmities.
And therefore we piously
in holy song are observing
your highly honored memorial,
and also extol you
as a treasury of healings and of God's almighty grace.

Verse: Blessed is the man who fears the Lord.

Joyful are all who love the devout,
having obtained an intercessor to God on high,
Anthimos, meek and blameless,
the cheerful monk who excelled
in ascetic labors on the holy mount
of Athos in recent times.
And they call to him, "Intercede
together with the Virgin ewe lamb and Mother of God;
for you always hymned

joyously her Entry into the Temple, since your residence
was named for this event.
So, we entreat you to join her
and pray to Christ God, the King of all,
to grant His great mercy
and His peace to those who in faith seek your assistance."

Glory. **Mode pl. 4.**

The Kingdom of Heaven is not for those who take it easy here, but for those who lead a life of much hardship and affliction. So saying, O thrice-blessed Anthimos, you prayed without ceasing and worked tiring, to obtain your daily bread. Therefore the Lord and King of all rewarded your labors for perfection, and He made you an heir of the joy and blessedness that never ends, and an unsleeping intercessor for us, who piously celebrate your ever-venerable memory.

Both now. **Theotokion.**

O Virgin who has not known man and yet ineffably conceived God in the flesh, Mother of the Most High God, accept entreaties from your supplicants, All-blameless one. To all you grant purification from their offenses. Do now accept our supplications, and entreat Him to save us all.

Now dismiss. Holy God, etc.

Apolytikion. Mode 3.

Special Melody: "Thy Confession of the Divine Faith"

With all reverence, let us praise Anthimos, who in our own time dawned over Athos like a star shedding a new light of piety as a brightly shining vessel of grace, bearing the undoubted flower of purity, with great love crying out to him: "As one who rejoices with the angels, ever entreat Christ for us."

Another Apolytikion.
Mode pl. 1. *Let us worship the Word.*

Let us duly extol the God-bearing Father,
the wise teacher and spiritual guide.
As the adornment of the Skete of St Anne,
the ancestor of God,
he is a light for Athonites,
and a spiritual guide for those who cry out to him:
"Father, entreat the Lord without ceasing
for us who honor you, O Anthimos."

Another Apolytikion
Same Melody

With melodious anthems let us extol the seed
of Kalliani that blossomed
in recent times in the Skete of Saint Anne
into a flower of ascetic life,

Anthimos, the guide of the faithful to perfection.
Let us say: "Since you are filled with the sweet aroma
of God, gladden us with the fragrance of your ardent
prayers."

Theotokion. Same Melody.

Rejoice, O impassable gate of God the Lord. Rejoice, wall
and shelter of those who take refuge in you. Rejoice,
stormless haven. O Maid who knew not man, yet physically
gave birth to your Creator and God. Never cease to intercede
for those who extol and worship the Son Whom you bore.

IX.
The Service of Matins
in honor of
our Devout and God-bearing
Father Anthimos of St. Anne's Skete

By Charalambos M. Bousias
Translated by Archimandrite Seraphim Dedes

Apolytikion. Mode 3.
Special Melody: "Thy Confession of the Divine Faith."

With all reverence, let us praise Anthimos, who in our own time dawned over Athos like a star shedding a new light of piety as a brightly shining vessel of grace, bearing the undoubted flower of purity, with great love crying out to him: "As one who rejoices with the angels, ever entreat Christ for us."

Kathisma I. Mode 1.
"The soldiers keeping watch."

With hymns let us extol the most wise,
God-inspired and modest,
meek confessor and Spiritual Father of holy cenobia,

our divine Father Anthimos.
For in recent times, he was distinguished for virtue
and ascetic feats,
and thus became the adornment
of the holy Skete of Saint Anne.

Glory. *Repeat.* Both now.
Theotokion.

The virtue-loving Anthimos religiously engaged in ascetic
endeavor in the Skete of your mother, Saint Anne,
as a resident in the house named for your divine Entry into
God's holy Temple, O all-pure Virgin, ever praising you,
the typological three-year-old heifer.

Kathisma II
Mode 4. *Go quickly before.*

You quieted turbulence at sea by your ardent prayer,
and cured the incurable and most distressing disease
of cancer, O Anthimos.
Therefore do we believers now with feeling extol you
as a shiny vessel of the Comforter;
and faced with hardships in our life,
we run to you for help.

Glory. *Repeat.* Both now.
Theotokion.

Most earnestly pray on our behalf to Christ your divine
and only-begotten Son, O Virgin Mother of God,
together with Anthimos,
our Father who has blossomed as a flower and offspring

of your sweet-smelling, fragrant, holy Garden on Athos,
entreating that all of us attain
the glory of God on high.

Kathisma III
Mode 3. *Seeing how beautiful.*

Let us extol in hymns the God-bearing Anthimos.
He was divinely wise; he was a guide of souls,
who lately rose up like a sun on Athos, that Holy Mountain.
He was very meek and pure; he was humble and innocent.
He did not own property; he was bright and dispassionate.
And let us shout to him in a loud voice:
Rejoice, O Spirit-bearing Father.

Glory. *Repeat.* Both now.
Theotokion.

O, Virgin Mary,
shine the light of the divine grace
of Christ, your Son and God
on my darkened soul;
for you, All-holy Lady,
are the hope of us who are hopeless.
Drive away the gloomy fog
of my sins that are numberless,
so that I might be absolved
and find mercy on Judgment Day.
With longing I unceasingly call out:
Rejoice, O Maiden full of grace.

The first Antiphon of Mode 4, and the Prokeimenon:

Precious in the sight of the Lord is the death of His saints.
Verse: Blessed is the man who fears the Lord.

The Holy Gospel according to Saint Luke (6:17-23).
See Friday of the second week of Saint Luke.
Psalm 50/51
Glory.

Through the prayers of Your saint, O Merciful One, blot out the multitude of our transgressions.
Now and ever.

Through the prayers of the Theotokos, O Merciful One, blot out the multitude of our transgressions.

Idiomelon, Mode pl. 2

Have mercy on me, O God, according to Your great goodness, and according to Your abundant mercy, blot out my transgressions. Jesus, having risen from the dead as He foretold, has given us eternal life and great mercy.

O Lord, save Your people and bless Your inheritance. Visit Your world with mercy and bounties, exalt the horn of Orthodox Christians, and send down upon us Your rich mercy.

The Canon

Ode 1 Mode 4. *I shall open my mouth.*

With honey-dripping odes,
let us extol the ascetic feats
of Anthimos who shone forth
upon Mount Athos of late.
Let us shout to him:
"Rejoice, O most resplendent
adornment of the Skete
of the divine Saint Anne."

We joyfully celebrate
your incorruptible way of life,
and honor you, Anthimos,
the holy Athonite monk and
truly God-inspired son of Kallianoi,
who lately received the crown
of immortality.

All-venerable Father Anthimos,
when you were only a boy of four,
you tasted the bitter cup
of your beloved mother's death.
Then you raised your hands
unto the Theotokos,
who stands as the heavenly
mother of all orphans.

Theotokion

O Mary, the all-wise guide
to perfection for all Christians,
you led your servant Father Anthimos,
guiding his way to your sweetest place,
your Garden on Mount Athos,
to find the delicious fruit
of holy theosis.

Ode 3. *Establish your servants.*

In Athens, O Father, the grace of the Ruler of all,
revealed to you a wise
director to angelic life,
the godly ascetic Jerome,
who like a tablet had inscribed
on him the rules of monastic life.

Displaying the decorum of monastics,
O Anthimos, tearfully you gave
yourself in obedience to Michael and Gabriel,
those brothers of a godly mind,
whom you reverently served.

When you made yourself a temple of the Comforter,
through discipline and ascetic feats,
O Father, in most recent years
on Athos, you distinguished yourself

in kindness and propriety,
O spirit-bearing Anthimos.

Theotokion

O Lady, higher than the Holy of Holies,
Anthimos, has lately arisen
as a great sun of virtue.
He always honored festively
your Entry into the Temple
as a three-year-old child,
O pure Virgin.

Mid-ode Kathisma
Mode 3. *Your confession of the divine Faith.*

Let us reverently extol our holy Father Anthimos,
that newly shining star of piety and vessel of divine grace,
who was a monk on Mount Athos in recent years,
a fragrant flower of learning and chastity.
Let us call out with longing,
"Since you now dwell with the Angels,
pray earnestly to Christ our God for us."

Glory. *Repeat.* Both now.
Theotokion.

You are highly praised, O Theotokos,
by the tempest-tossed, as their safe haven,
and the mightiest protector of celibates.

The Holy Mountain has you as its guardian,
and Christian peoples have you as their pride and joy.
We entreat you now, O Lady, from heaven send to us
your Son and God's abundant grace and great mercy.

Ode 4. *He who sits in holy glory.*

O all-honored Anthimos,
the adornment and glory
of the God-bearing Fathers of Athos,
with the sprinkling of your intercessions
you sanctify those who extol you in song
and for the sake of whom you expended yourself,
for their perfection in Christ our God.

With the eyes of your soul you gazed on the Lord,
and chanted ceaselessly to Him
even in your deep old age.
Standing upright before Him while serving as a priest,
you would shine like the sun, O blessed Anthimos.

As a pearl of true discernment
and the store of humility,
treasure of forbearance,
and the rule and standard of diligence,
you looked askance on mundane affairs as rubbish ,
O wise Anthimos,
and sought that which will not perish.

Theotokion

Holy Virgin, bright as sunshine,
Father Anthimos did possess
the most holy icon
of your sacred Entry into the Lord's
all-holy Temple, as inviolate wealth;
he extolled you each day,
and he would run for help to your grace.

Ode 5. *Amazed was the universe.*

O wise Father Anthimos,
you comforted the men who came
to your humble dwelling with your counsels
and words of wisdom;
for you had truly become
a God-inspired river of wisdom,
and an ever-flowing stream
of God's love to your fellow-man.
You tasted the bitterness of orphanage in childhood,
and your cruel step-mother's ill-treatment.
So at a young age, you left your father's house,
and went to Mount Athos, where you found
a sweet refuge for yourself,
O devout Father Anthimos.

You followed most recently
the trodden path bequeathed to us
by the holy Fathers of the desert.

So to your eyes
you gave no slumber or sleep,
but said that the Kingdom of God
is taken by forceful men,
O thrice-blessed Father Anthimos.

Theotokion

O Lady, who knew not man,
lately a very fragrant bloom
blossomed in your Garden on Mount Athos,
the God-illumined ascetic Anthimos,
the lover of all virtues, who each day
magnified you piously,
and extolled you in hymns of praise.

Ode 6. *Let us possessed.*

Through fasting, tears, and unceasing prayer,
you made your heart a grand and magnificent
Temple for God on high,
O most devout Father Anthimos,
and you received the honor of incorruption.

You were a brilliant torch of theology, O Anthimos,
enlightened by the rays of the will of God,
a flashing beacon and guiding light,
illumining the darkness
for all who came to you.

O jewel of monks, Father Anthimos,
like a most beautiful bird, you flew to
unutterable heights of virtue, patience, obedience,
humility, discernment,
and ultimately love.

Theotokion

Your servant Anthimos led his life
soberly and in chastity, O Mother.
As we now sing his praise,
we all unceasingly honor you,
as the brightest lamp of virginity, O Virgin.

Kontakion.
Mode plagal 4.
Special Melody: "O Victorious Leader"

As a most enlightened and inspired ascetic, a follower of the
way of stillness and wakefulness, let us praise the newly
planted yet undoubted fragrant Flower of the Holy
Mountain, a Rose of the great Skete of Saint Anne, with great
love crying out, "Hail, most wise Anthimos."

To the illumined and Spirit-filled ascetic, to the practitioner
of watchfulness and stillness, to the very fragrant rose of the
Skete of Saint Anne, who has sprung forth on the Holy
Mountain latterly as its sweetest blossom, let us sing hymns

of praise, and with longing exclaim: Rejoice, most wise Anthimos.

Oikos.

Anthimos, blessed Father, you were seen on Mount Athos as a flower of God's holy wisdom; for having gone about your own life laboriously, you became an excellent guide to heaven for monastics. And now from earth you hear us saying:

Rejoice, the offspring of Kallianoi;
Rejoice, the glory of monastics.
Rejoice, for you had the zeal of the ancient Fathers;
Rejoice, for you associate with the holy angels.
Rejoice, book of divine knowledge and of fatherly love;
Rejoice, consecrated house of obedience in Christ.
Rejoice, for you have honored the Skete of Saint Anne;
Rejoice, for you have carried humility's banner.
Rejoice, the rule of prayer and gentleness;
Rejoice, for you indeed attained theosis.
Rejoice, the leader of devout monastics.
Rejoice, director of many Christians.
Rejoice, most wise Anthimos.

Synaxarion

On this day, June 15, is the memorial of our venerable and God-bearing Father Anthimos, who in the recent past lived in ascetic discipline, dear to God, in the Holy Skete of Saint Anne [on the Holy Mountain, Athos], and was the clairvoyant Spiritual Father of countless pious Orthodox Christians.

Couplet

All-blessed Anthimos, you recently shone forth
as a fragrant flower of superior wisdom.
At his holy intercession,
O Christ God, have mercy on us and save us. Amen.

Ode 7. *Godly-minded three.*

Sweetest Anthimos,
we honor you with hymns today
as one who loved to pray,
as one who guarded with care
his bodily senses all,
and as the enemy
of the Evil One,
and as a close and loyal friend
of Jesus, the Giver of Life.

O blessed Anthimos,
with inspired words and counsels
you refreshed the souls of those who came to you on Athos,
where you resided, O Saint,
and in the Skete of Saint Anne,
the holy grandmother of God,
in your Kalyva, named for the Entry of the Virgin.

O blessed Anthimos,
your venerable face was bright
with godly cheerfulness,
your mouth produced holy words,
like nectar and honey from
the rock, for you were full
of benevolence,
like sweetest nectar, dripping it
on the souls of the faithful.

Theotokion

Virgin Mother of God,
the high-as-heaven cypress tree
of true virginity,
at the entreaties and prayers
of Anthimos, make our thoughts
and feelings heavenly,
and enable us
to always seek the higher things
in this life, as we extol you.

Ode 8. *The Pious Children.*

The Creator of creation was pleased
by your holy life and your ascetic ways.
O Father Anthimos,
laity and celibates were gladdened

by the sweetness of your fragrant way of life;
for you had blossomed forth on Mount Athos,
in the very great Skete of Saint Anne,
as pleasant jasmine.

Holy Father Anthimos,
you were distinguished in virtue;
thus you were an immovable
pillar of civility, and of never-ceasing prayer,
and knowledge of the Lord's commands.
Having foretold the time of your demise,
you were then translated to heavenly dwellings
to be with Christ forever.

As the chosen vessel of the Comforter,
you knew in advance whatever was to come to pass,
O Anthimos, and you saw into souls;
for, deadening the action of your body's senses
you roused the movements of your internal senses,
glorifying Jesus, as Saint Isaac the Syrian affirms.

Theotokion

Blameless ever-virgin Theotokos,
we pray that your intercessions are protecting us,
so that we, your suppliants,
guarded round about by them,
might trample on the cunning schemes
of our demonic foes,

and thus attain the height of immortal
glory, where the choirs
of saints are celebrating.

Ode 9. *All you born on earth.*

Anthimos, you found
an entrance to contemplation
in the active life.
Therefore in the meadow of
the Theotokos you worked with diligence
to cultivate your gardens and
to keep a tidy house;
and you labored
as an iconographer,
painting icons of saints, O venerable one.

Since you kept the Lord's
commandments entirely,
you drew unto yourself
the grace of the All-Holy Spirit;
and God the Word made you into a true physician
and philosopher, even a scientist,
even though you lacked a formal secular
education, O God-bearing Anthimos.

Father, you preserved intact
the dogmas and canons of
the holy Faith,

for they were your pride and joy.
For you the sweetest pleasure in life for you
was to study them religiously.
And thus in recent years,
O all-wise one,
you were a most brilliant star
of the Orthodox mindset, O Anthimos.

Theotokion

Mary, Queen of all,
the thrice-blessed Anthimos
rejoices forevermore
in that never-ending joy, with you,
O glorious Mother of our God.
That hoary and all-venerable
Elder and Athonite
was a recent lover and enthusiast
of the blameless religion of Christ your Son.

Exaposteilarion
Mode 2. *O Women hearken.*

To Anthimos let us sing hymns
of praise, for he was Spirit-filled.
He was a sweet-scented flower
within the Skete of St. Anne.
And lately he delighted all
creation with the fragrance of
his undefiled way of life;
for he was a rose of insight
and a pure lily of foresight.

Theotokion. Same Melody.

O blessed Lady, you conceived
the King of glory in your womb,
and thus became Theotokos
ineffably and delivered
humanity from burdensome
dishonor. At the fervent prayers
of godly-minded Anthimos,
deliver us from the madness
of the malevolent Belial.

Stichera on the Praises
Mode 1. *For the celestial orders.*

Heeding the words and the teachings
of the blind Michael
and his illumined brother,
Father Gabriel Lambis,
you ran with godly wisdom the sacred race
of ascetical discipline,
O Father Anthimos, finishing at the peak
of the virtues, which are hard to attain.

Longing for eternal glory,
you kept yourself aloof
from all mundane attachments,
O devout one, and followed
Jesus, the Creator, through actions of love,

patience, fasting and ardent prayer;
O Father Anthimos, He then rewarded you
and He glorified you worthily.

The grace of foresight was given
to you by God as a gift
from heaven, thus confirming
your impeccable lifestyle.
Thereby you revealed what was known to no one,
and astounded your visitors.
You were a treasure of virtue at Saint Anne's Skete,
O ascetic Father Anthimos.

Let us who love the monastic saints
extol Anthimos,
who recently shone forth wondrously on Mount Athos.
He was an unerring spiritual guide
and a fragrant receptacle
of the ineffable wisdom that comes from God.
Let us dutifully honor him.

Glory.

Mode pl. 1.

O venerable God-bearing Father Anthimos, you followed in the steps of the Fathers, who of old were illumined by God; and you led a life that emulated the angels, on Athos in recent times. As a child, you tasted the bitterness of being an orphan, and you never knew a mother's tender love; and yet you became a sweet and tender-loving spiritual father, O godly-minded one. Therefore, you became famous, and you were respected by all. Then, you departed to your Lord, whom you had loved throughout your life. And now we pray you entreat Him earnestly, asking that He save our souls.

Both now. **Theotokion.**

We pronounce you blessed, O Virgin Theotokos,
and we glorify you, duty-bound as believers;
the unshakable city, the indestructible wall,
the firm and steadfast protection,
and place of refuge for our souls.

The Great Doxology and the Dismissal

X.

Supplicatory Canon
to our Devout and God-bearing
Father Anthimos of St. Anne's Skete

By Charalambos M. Bousias
Translated by Archimandrite Seraphim Dedes

The Priest says "Blessed is our God". Psalm 142 *is read.*
Then the following is chanted in the usual manner.

God is the Lord, and He appeared to us. Blessed is He who comes in the name of the Lord. (4)

Mode 4. *You who were lifted.*

When you received the grace of God, O devout one,
then you became a guide to heavenly mansions
for Orthodox believers. As a God-illumined man,
you became a temple of
godly wisdom, O Father Anthimos.
And therefore we entreat you to cease not
your earnest intercession with the Lord,
for us who faithfully honor your memory.

Glory. *Repeat.* Both now.

Theotokion.

We who are unworthy shall never refrain,
from proclaiming your powers, O Theotokos.
For were you not concerned to intercede for us,
who would have delivered us
from such manifold dangers,
and who else would up to now
have preserved us in freedom?
O Lady, we shall not depart from you,
for you ever save your servants
from evils of every kind.

Psalm 50, *then the Canon.*
Ode 1. Mode pl. 4. *Of old when the Israelite.*

I call to you, Anthimos blessed Saint,
to drive out the darkness
that befuddles my feeble mind,
and gloomy depression from my poor soul,
by your entreaties that flash like a lightning bolt.

You deadened carnality in yourself
through ascetic practice.
By humility and by prayer
you received the gift of interceding
for us who worthily honor you, Anthimos.

From God you received the ability
to fill the requests of

those who run to your holy prayers.
We ask you to give us all the power
to walk the hard path of life without reproach.

Theotokion.

O Lady, enable us to destroy
every machination
of the Enemy of our souls;
also, by your holy intercession,
grant us the power to trample his insolence.

Ode 3. *O divine Master Builder.*

For the monks of Mount Athos
you are the new guiding light.
Drive away the fog of the troubles and pains besetting us.
In recent years the rays
of all your virtues illumined
pious people everywhere,
wise Father Anthimos.

The divine Skete of Saint Anne
holds you in highest esteem,
as do all the Athonite fathers,
O Elder of the Church.
Enable me to walk
the way of all God's commandments,
by your intercessory
prayers to the King of all.

In your time on Mount Athos,
you replicated the feats
of the great ascetics before you,
O blessed Anthimos.
And therefore you received
the grace of God in abundance,
to rid us of every base
passion that brings us down.

Theotokion.

You, O Lady, are honored
in every language of man,
for you are the all-holy Mother
of the all-merciful
Lord God and King of all;
you are the only all-blessed
and pure virgin Mother,
who are ever extolled by all.

Deliver us
from all mistreatment and dark trouble that the devil
wreaks on us who with longing sing
your praises, O Anthimos;
and pray to the Lord for us with great earnest.

Look graciously
upon your servant, all-praiseworthy Theotokos,
and upon my painful physical suffering,
and remedy my anguish of spirit.

Litany, then the Kathisma.
Kathisma.Mode 2. *In seeking the heights.*

You are the new guiding light of monks , O Anthimos,
who shone with the light of every virtue splendidly.
Drive away the ignorance
and the darkness of troubles from us who run
to you, who gladdened all with your advice
and wisdom that truly was inspired by God.

Ode 4. *I have heard.*

Most holy priest, Father Anthimos,
keep us all uninjured by the attacks on us
of our spiritual enemies,
for we flee to your unfailing patronage.

By your prayers to the Lord, dispel
from us all the stench of our sinful way of life,
as a fragrant flower, Anthimos,
of Mount Athos, as your holy name denotes.

Subordinate to the divine law
all the uncontrollable movements of my flesh,
Father Anthimos, and raise my mind
to the Lord, with whom you now rejoice on high.

Theotokion.

Holy Mother of God, give not
slumber to the spiritual eyels of my soul,
lest the diabolic Enemy
shoot me with his deadly darts and injure me.

Ode 5. *Sovereign Lord.*

Calm the surging waves
of distress for all who run to you
and take refuge in your prayers to the Lord,
and direct our life in peace, O revered Anthimos.

Now we, the hosts of the Orthodox who honor you,
run to your divine protection and your help
when in danger, O thrice-blessed Father Anthimos.

From the heavens' heights,
O Father Anthimos, direct our life
in the way the true fear of God,
which you had as your companion
throughout your life.

Theotokion.

Set your ardent prayers,
Theotokos, like a mighty wall
that surrounds us, so that guarded in their camp
we may all remain unharmed by life's adversities.

Ode 6. *My prayer.*

O Anthimos, drive away the gloomy fog
of the suffering and straights that beset us;
we now entreat you, O Father, who traveled
the straight and narrow way, leading a blameless life,
which brought you all the way to Christ
and the luminous mansions of God on high.

Invisibly from the heights bestow understanding on me,
and enlighten your children to know and do
what will properly lead us
along the ways of theosis, O Anthimos,
and to the never-ending joy.
You yourself never cease to rejoice with Christ.

In recent times, having raised your mind's desire
to the Lord on high, and being illumined
by light divine, you were truly distinguished
in word and deed on Mount Athos, O Anthimos.
And thus to heavenly abodes
you directed the people who came to you.

Theotokion.

The love of God and His kindness dwell in you,
Theotokos. Therefore we, who extol you,
pray you to help in guarding our senses,
through which, like windows, the devil invades our souls.
And his attacks will be repelled

when we have your assistance in fighting him.

Deliver us
from all mistreatment and dark trouble that the devil
wreaks on us who with longing sing
your praises, O Anthimos;
and pray to the Lord for us with great earnest.

Entreat for us, O spotless Maiden,
who ineffably gave birth to the divine Word
through a word in the latter days,
since you indeed
speak with maternal boldness.

Litany, then the Kontakion.
Kontakion. Mode 2. *Using the streams.*

You were an excellent teacher of piety;
you were adorned with obedience and gentleness,
O God-bearing Father, Saint Anthimos.
You gladdened the faithful in teaching them,
and comforted all with your holy words.

Prokeimenon.

Precious in the sight of the Lord is the death of His saint.
Verse: Blessed is the man who fears the Lord.

The reading is from the *Holy Gospel* according to Matthew.
(11:27-30)

The Lord said to his disciples, "All things have been delivered to me by my Father; and no one knows the Son except the Father, and no one knows the Father except the Son and any one to whom the Son chooses to reveal him. Come to me, all who labor and are heavy laden, and I will give you rest. Take my yoke upon you, and learn from me; for I am gentle and lowly in heart, and you will find rest for your souls. For my yoke is easy, and my burden is light."

Glory.

At the intercession of Your devout one, O merciful Lord, blot out my many offenses.

Both now.

At the intercessions of the Theotokos, O merciful Lord, blot out my many offenses.

Prosomoion.

Verse: Have mercy on me, O God, according to your steadfast love; according to your abundant mercy blot out my transgression.

Mode pl. 2. *When the saint deposited.*

Holy Father Anthimos,
you are the new luminary
of the holy Church of Christ,

and the shining beacon
of the Holy Mountain.
You gave light to the souls
of all who approached you
and took refuge in your sound advice,
by the unwaning light
of your bright and God-loving way of life
and your ascetic discipline,
which you followed zealously day and night.
Therefore we entreat you,
the jewel of monastics, to send down
on us the mercies of Christ our God,
by your mighty prayers to Him.

O God, save Your people…
Ode 7. *The Children from Judea.*

As the gem of devotion
and the vessel of foresight,
the sacred instrument
of insight, rouse your children
to holy acquisition
of things higher, O Anthimos.
They honor you and they seek
your ardent intercession.

With melodious anthems
we have crowned your divine and
resplendent memory,
O Anthimos, the jewel
of Athonite Fathers,

and we ask you to beautify
our minds with thoughts that are pure
and blameless recollections.

On behalf of your children
who extol you, with earnest
entreat the Savior Christ;
for you can speak directly
to Him who has compassion,
God-illumined Saint Anthimos,
spiritual guide of a host
of the devout Christians.

Theotokion.

The protection and shelter
of all Christians, O Virgin,
and holy guardian
of Holy Mountain Athos,
be quick to hear the voices
of the prayers of us who extol
and glorify your divine
and all-glorious Son.

Ode 8. *O praise and bless Him.*

You are a rain cloud
of prayers, O Anthimos. Therefore,
from on high pour down showers, bestowing

health of soul and body
on all of us, O Father.

Give me the power
against the devil's deceptions,
you who spat on his pride, holy Father,
through ascetic practice,
prayer and humility.

By your petitions
to Christ our Lord and Redeemer,
cure my soul, which is sick, I entreat you,
Anthimos our Father,
new oracle of heaven.

Theotokion.

Anoint your servants
with the perfume of your prayers,
O Mother and Vessel of perfume
of the King of all,
we praise you with divine hymns.

Ode 9. *You are the Theotokos.*

O Anthimos of Athos,
new devout ascetic,
we who take refuge in you pray you never cease
to intercede for us daily

with the Almighty God.

O Anthimos, the model
of divine obedience,
the rock of vigilance, now we extol the pains
you took attaining dispassion
and gaining theosis.

From ignorance to knowledge
lead me, holy Father,
being the servant of Christ God, O Anthimos,
unerring guide to salvation
for all the faithful.

Theotokion.

O Mary Theotokos, highly favored one,
I pray you wash my unclean and defiled heart,
using my tears of repentance,
that I may sing your praise.

Megalynaria

It is truly meet to call you blest, O Theotokos, the ever-blessed and all-blameless one, and the Mother of our God. Greater in honor than the Cherubim, and in glory greater beyond compare than the Seraphim, you without corruption gave birth to God the Word, and are truly Theotokos, you do we magnify.

Man of God and God-bearing man, rejoice,
paragon of wisdom,
filled with light of the Triune God;
many called you their Spiritual Father,
and teacher of the true faith,
all-honored Anthimos.

Anthimos, imbued with the Spirit's grace,
teacher of the faithful
with a God-pleasing way of life,
God-illumined guide of
monastics and the married,
rejoice, O fragrant bloom of
virtue and holiness.

Recently you filled the entire world
with the fragrant scent of
your most virtuous way of life.
We who now extol you,
Saint Anthimos, entreat you
to drive away the stench of
passions and ignorance.

Rejoice newly shining lamp of the Church;
son of Kalliani
and the product and sacred height
of the Holy Mountain,
who lately shone in wisdom
and in ascetic virtues,
O all-wise Anthimos.

Anthimos, you shone forth in recent years
as a brilliant pillar
of sobriety, and a sweet -sounding harp of goodness,
a paragon of holy obedience, a shining
lantern of self-control.

Anthimos, the keeper of all the Lord's
commandments, the fixed and
shining star of practical love,
is the latest standard
of Spirit-bearing Fathers of Athos.
Let us therefore sing hymns of praise to him.

All you arrays of angelic powers
and the Forerunner of the Lord,
the holy twelve Apostles and all the Saints,
together with the Theotokos,
intercede for us now,
that we may all be saved.

Holy God, etc.
Apolytikion. Mode pl. 1. *Let us worship the Word.*

Let us duly extol him, the burning torch of love,
devout and God-bearing Father,
a teacher holy and wise,
and the jewel of the Skete of God's ancestor Anne.
He is for Athonites a light
and a spiritual guide

of us who address him: "Father,
entreat the Lord without ceasing
for us who honor you, O Anthimos."

Litany *and* **Dismissal**, *after which we chant the following:*
Mode 2. *When he took you.*

Blessed Father Anthimos, fulfill
all requests of those who entreat you
to pray to God for them.
Grant the final victory over the devil to us
who extol you with faith and love,
O model of virtue.
Most distinguished Athonite,
the cheerful look on your face
gladdened the entire Holy Mountain
and the holy Skete of Saint Anne,
the esteemed ancestor of Christ our God.

Lady, receive the supplications of your servants,
 and rescue us from all necessity and affliction.

Mother of God, I have committed my every hope entirely to
you. Keep me under your shelter.

Couplet

Anthimos, accept the supplication of Charalambos,
as translated by one angelic in name only.

GLOSSARY OF TERMS

Arsanas: A pier, or landing place for boats, with warehouses and other buildings.

Ascetic: A person engaged in a life of spiritual endeavor, which includes prayer, fasting, keeping vigil, etc. Also, a monastic saint (hosios) distinguished for his life of striving for holiness.

Ascesis: Spiritual struggle, or training of soul and body, which leads to spiritual regeneration. It consists of purifying the soul of all the vices, and acquiring all the virtues through the grace of God.

Dikaios: A monk chosen to preside over the affairs of a skete for the term of one year. He deals with the administrative and spiritual problems of the Skete. In particular, he assumes the expenses of offering hospitality to the pilgrims.

Epitrachelion: Priestly vestment worn around the neck.

Hagioritic: Pertaining to the Holy (hagion) Mountain (oros), Mount Athos.

Hagarenes: Decendents of Hagar, Abraham's concubine (Genesis 16, Galatians 4:22-31). This term usually refers to Moslems.

Hesychastyrion: A hermitage.

Hieromonk: A monk who has been ordained to the holy priesthood.

Kalyva: A small isolated cottage with a chapel.

Kenosis: Self-emptying. Primarily used to describe the Son emptying Himself (Phil. 2:6) when He became man.

Lavra: A large monastery with many monks. Originally, the term signified a group of individual cells around a church and trapeza.

Metochion: A dependency of a monastery. Also, a parish church of one of the national Orthodox Churches located on the territory of another. It is sometimes known as a representation church.

Nipsis: Inner wakefulness, an active state of mind which frees the heart and mind of distracting thoughts, images, and passions. It is a prerequisite for interior prayer of the heart.

Noetic: Belonging to the intellect (nous), the highest faculty in man.

Panagia: The All-holy Mother of God, the Virgin Mary.

Pascha: The Feast of the Lord's Resurrection.

Passions: Evil feelings, emotions, or inclinations which do not function according to the purpose for which God gave them to man.

Rudder: A book containing the Canons of the Seven Holy Ecumenical Synods, and those of various regional synods. The Orthodox Church is governed by the holy canons, which deal with doctrinal and administrative matters. This collection of canons is called *The Rudder* because it corresponds to the rudder of a ship, which guides the vessel on its course.

Skete: Settlement of hermits near a common church (kyriakon) where they gather on Sundays and Feast days for common worship. It is also a monastic settlement without the autonomy of a monastery.

Theosis: "Deification" or "divinization," union with God through His divine energies.

Theotokos: She who gave birth to God, the Virgin Mary.

Trapeza: The dining area in a monastery, or the communal meal served there.

Vice: Passions which have become habitual or fixed character traits. They are a sign of the soul's ugliness and diseased condition.

Virtue: Beautiful qualities of the soul. They are a sign of spiritual health.

Vyrona: A suburb of northeastern Athens.